P9-BAW-081

C. S. LEWIS

THE MAN BEHIND NARNIA

C. S. Lewis

The Man Behind Narnia

✤ ✤ ✤ ✤

Beatrice Gormley

Eerdmans Books for Young Readers
Grand Rapids, Michigan / Cambridge, U.K.

© 1998 by Beatrice Gormley
This edition published 2005 by
Eerdmans Books for Young Readers
an imprint of Wm. B. Eerdmans Publishing Company
255 Jefferson Ave. S.E., Grand Rapids, Michigan 49503
P.O. Box 163, Cambridge CB3 9PU U.K.
www.eerdmans.com/youngreaders

All rights reserved
Printed in the United States of America

05 06 07 08 09 10   7 6 5 4 3 2

Library of Congress Cataloging-in-Publication Data

Gormley, Beatrice.
C.S. Lewis : the man behind Narnia / written by Beatrice Gormley.
-- 2nd ed.
p. cm.
Rev. ed. of: C.S. Lewis : Christian and storyteller. 1998.
Includes bibliographical references and index.
ISBN 0-8028-5301-3 (alk. paper)
1. Lewis, C. S. (Clive Staples), 1898-1963--Juvenile literature.
2. Authors, English--20th century--Biography--Juvenile literature.
3. Anglicans--England--Biography--Juvenile literature. 4. Christian
biography--England--Juvenile literature. 5. Church of England
--Biography--Juvenile literature. 6. Narnia (Imaginary place)
--Juvenile literature.   I. Title.
PR6023.E926Z6643 2005
823'.912--dc22
[B]

2005007914

Cover photograph by Burt Glinn, courtesy of Magnum Photos, Inc.

In memory of my grandfather
The Reverend Herbert H. Fisher
— B. G.

CONTENTS

❖ ❖ ❖ ❖

INTRODUCTION

ONE DAY IN 1929, in Oxford, England, a man got on a bus. This man, C. S. Lewis, was a teaching fellow at Oxford University and a brilliant scholar. Ever since he was a young boy, he had wanted to be a great poet, but not many people knew about that. His students were in awe of his "sheer intellectual power." His best friends, even the ones who relished a hard-fought debate, felt that arguing with Lewis was like fighting a howitzer with a peashooter.

Ten years earlier, when C. S. Lewis came to Oxford as a student, he had been an atheist — one who does not believe in God. Slowly and reluctantly he had decided that there must be some sort of spiritual force behind the universe — but certainly not a God who took a personal interest in him. Now, sitting in the top of the double-decker bus, he had the feeling that he must make an all-important choice.

For a long, long time, he realized, he had been "shutting

something out." He had been going around with his defenses up, as if he were wearing a suit of armor or — less dignified — as if he were a lobster. Now he saw that he had a choice: he could take the risk of dropping his defenses. He could finally let in the "something" he had worked so hard at shutting out — God.

Two years later, C. S. Lewis joined the Christian church. From that point on, he considered his Christian faith the most important thing in his life. Other people might admire him as a remarkable teacher, public speaker, and author, but Lewis thought the most important thing about him was the belief he shared with millions of others.

To C. S. Lewis, Christianity was a matter of life and death — eternal life and eternal death. There was a real hell and devils, a real heaven and angels. God was not some vague, distant Supreme Being. He was like a magnificent lion, like Aslan in Lewis's Narnia books, breathing right in your face.

Some readers enjoy Lewis's books *in spite of* his Christianity, trying to ignore it or explain it away. This would make him smile — as a young man, he did the same thing with his favorite authors who were Christian. But the Christianity in Lewis's writing is not something extra; it is woven into the fabric of his books. Without his faith, he could not have written them.

Once Lewis opened the door to God, he began to write with a new understanding. He had struggled and worried over the poems he had hoped would make him a great poet, but now he wrote quickly and easily. He wrote essays and books explaining Christian beliefs; he wrote novels that combined science fiction and fantasy with spiritual adventure. And he wrote seven children's books, the Chronicles of Narnia.

Unlike many adults, Lewis respected children's books as

much as he respected scholarly dissertations or theological tomes. At the age of fifty he still read children's books for his own enjoyment. "I don't think age matters so much as people think," he wrote a few years later, after his first children's book had been published. "Parts of me are still twelve, and I think other parts were already fifty when I was twelve."

Many people assume that C. S. Lewis wrote the Chronicles of Narnia in order to send children moral Christian messages. But Lewis said he had no such intention when he began to write the Narnia stories. *After* he had written them, he saw that they might make Christian ideas "for the first time appear in their real potency" by setting them in an imaginary world, stripped of "their stained-glass and Sunday school associations." He was certain that it would be foolish for him or any other adult to preach down to children. "We have been told on high authority [Jesus' teaching in the Gospel according to Luke] that in the moral sphere they are probably at least as wise as we."

Besides, Lewis explained, moralizing is the wrong way to write stories. The author's job is to tell a story as well as he or she can. If there is to be any moral, it will "rise from whatever spiritual roots you have succeeded in striking during the whole course of your life."

So deep were C. S. Lewis's spiritual roots, and so intertwined with his work, that readers get a vivid sense of the man himself from his stories. In that way, his stories are like his letters. "You opened the envelope and you heard his voice," his close friend Owen Barfield once said. And when you open one of C. S. Lewis's books, he speaks to you — you hear his voice.

Lewis as a baby

CHAPTER 1

"HE IS JACKSIE"

WHEN HE WAS ABOUT four years old, Clive Staples Lewis took a dislike to his first name. One day, according to his older brother, Warren, "he marched up to my mother, put a forefinger on his chest, and announced, 'He is Jacksie.' He stuck to this the next day and thereafter, refusing to answer to any other name." "Jacksie" eventually became "Jack," which would be Lewis's name to his family and close friends for the rest of his life.

A picture of Jack at about this age shows a chubby-faced boy in a sailor suit, leading a toy Father Christmas on a toy donkey. This picture sums up Jack in a happy, confident stage of his childhood. For the most part, life was good. If some part of his life, such as his given name, did not seem good, then perhaps he could change it.

Jack's parents both grew up in Belfast, now the capital of Northern Ireland. His father, Albert Lewis, was a lawyer, the son of a Belfast shipbuilder and boilermaker. Flora Hamilton Lewis, Jack's

C. S. Lewis at four, about the
age when he announced to
his mother, "He is Jacksie"

mother, was the daughter of the Reverend Thomas Hamilton, vicar
of the church that Albert and his family attended. She was especially
talented in mathematics and had a degree from Queen's College,
Belfast. Albert fell in love with Flora Hamilton shortly after he began practicing law in Belfast, but he had to woo her for several years
before she agreed to marry him.

In 1894, Flora and Albert were married by her father at St.
Mark's, Dundela (a suburb of Belfast), where Thomas Hamilton was
vicar. The newly-wed Lewises settled down to family life in a small
rented house on the outskirts of the prosperous city of Belfast. Their
first son, Warren Hamilton Lewis, was born on June 16, 1895. On
November 29, 1898, the son they named Clive Staples Lewis came

into the world.

Like other middle-class families, the Lewises had servants: a cook, a maid, a gardener, and a nursemaid (later a governess) for Jack and his brother. Looking back, Jack considered the two great blessings of his early life to be his brother and his nursemaid, Lizzie. "As nearly as a human can be, simply good," he described her later.

Sometimes Mr. Lewis would lift one of the boys onto his back and carry him down to the docks. Ships were constantly coming and going in the harbor, since Belfast was a center of industry and a busy port. Both Jack and Warnie (Jack's brother's nickname), as well as Mr. Lewis, liked to draw ships, and ships figured in the stories and games that Jack and Warnie shared. One picture drawn by Jack shows a ship under full sail, manned by mice.

Much of the time, Jack and his brother were not allowed to play outdoors. In the early 1900s, a worry for parents was tuberculosis, a deadly disease that was thought to be caused by cold and dampness. When it rained (as it often does in Ireland), children were kept inside. Jack would gaze out the nursery window at the green Castlereagh Hills nearby as if they were a far-off fabled land.

In addition to playing indoors, the boys didn't go to school; they were tutored at home. Their mother taught them French and Latin, and a governess taught them other subjects such as arithmetic.

Although Jack and Warnie spent a great deal of time at home, indoors, they had no trouble amusing themselves. The boys knew other children, cousins and neighbors, but most of the time they were each other's only companions. Even though he was three years younger than Warnie, Jack was still bright and assertive enough to keep up with his older brother. They became close friends.

The Lewis brothers often spent rainy days writing stories

and plays and drawing pictures to go with them. They developed their own private world, to which Jack's contribution was a medieval country, peopled by talking creatures, called "Animal-Land."

At the age of six or seven, Jack completed a three-act play, *The King's Ring*. This was an unusual accomplishment for so young a child — never mind that the spelling was a bit erratic. Jack's play featured such "interesting carictars" as Bunny, King of Animal-Land (modeled on the boys' toy rabbit), and Sir Big, a "world-famed gentleman" frog. The dialogue shows that Jack's love of medieval times began early:

> SIR PETER (to King Bunny): Know you the
> bar-man's name?
> KING BUNNY: His name is Hit.
> GOLD FISH: T'is an odd one in sooth, how
> came you know it your Magasty?
> KING BUNNY: I heard folk call him Hit.

In his autobiography, *Surprised by Joy* (published when he was middle-aged), Jack explained that he took to writing as a child because he was too clumsy to build things with his hands. He *was* clumsy, both as a child and as an adult, because of the odd fact that the top joints of his thumbs didn't bend. But more to the point, Jack's imagination was extraordinarily vivid.

If Jack pictured a scene in his mind, it was as if he had really been there and really met the people of that place. Even as a child, he had a gift for storytelling. A cousin of Jack and Warnie's later remembered playing in a black oak wardrobe, the one hand-carved by their grandfather. The three children would crawl into the wardrobe and huddle there in the dark while Jack told stories.

Flora Hamilton Lewis   Albert Lewis

Neither Mr. nor Mrs. Lewis liked fantasy — they never "listened to the horns of elfland," as Jack put it in *Surprised by Joy*. Still, Jack's own love of fantasy was encouraged from the beginning by his nursemaid. Lizzie read Jack and Warnie "The Three Bears" and other fairy tales, and she told them Irish legends and folktales.

Although Jack's vivid imagination gave him much pleasure, it was so intense that it sometimes overwhelmed him. And the frightening side of his imagination was just as real to him as the enjoyable side. "When I was young," wrote Jack years later, to one of the readers of his Narnia books, "all my dreams were horrors — insects the size of small ponies which closed in upon me, etc."

Jack's powerful imagination could also lead him astray. For instance, he was fascinated by Lizzie's story about a crock of gold buried at the end of the rainbow. One day, Jack and Warnie thought they could see exactly where the rainbow ended: in the middle of

Little Lea, where Jack and his older brother, Warnie, grew up

the front walk. They dug a large hole in the walk — without finding any gold — and then it got dark and it was time to go indoors. A little later Mr. Lewis, coming home from his office, fell into the hole and accused the boys of digging it deliberately to trip him. Jack tried to explain about the crock of gold, but his father doubted that even young boys like Jack and Warnie could actually believe such a legend.

One of the pure pleasures of Jack's childhood was the summers he spent at the seashore. Every year, from the time Jack was a toddler, Mrs. Lewis rented a house at a resort on the coast of Northern Ireland. Warnie, Jack, their mother, and the nursemaid took a horse-drawn cab to the Belfast train station, and then rode the train to Castlerock or another seaside resort.

Mr. Lewis, however, stayed in Belfast and worked. Although

he dearly loved his wife and children, he had the temperament of a worrier, and he felt more comfortable in the unchanging routine of his office and home. Once in a while he would join the family for a weekend, but it was hard for him to tear himself away from his work and relax for even a few days. "I can still see him on his occasional visits to the seaside," wrote Warren many years later, "walking moodily up and down the beach, hands in trouser pockets, eyes on the ground, every now and then giving a heartrending yawn and pulling out his watch."

To Jack and Warnie, the seaside vacation was the high point of the year. Jack loved the water, and he would delight in swimming, or even just dunking himself in water, for the rest of his life. A friend remembered swimming with Jack in the ocean when they were both middle-aged; he described Jack as "a strong swimmer, playing in and out of the rollers like a dolphin, undeterred by cold."

✛ ✛ ✛ ✛

In 1905 the Lewises had a house built in Leeborough, a suburb of Belfast, farther into the country than their first home. Their large new brick house, named "Little Lea," was three stories high, with bay windows in front and several chimneys.

Warren later judged that the house was poorly designed and built, with much wasted space. But when he and Jack were boys, they were thrilled with all the hideaways and crannies. "To a child it seemed less like a house than a city," wrote Jack in his autobiography. ". . . I am a product of long corridors, empty sunlit rooms, upstairs indoor silences, attics explored in solitude, distant noises of gurgling cisterns and pipes, and the noise of wind under the [roof] tiles."

Jack's life at Little Lea would have been almost perfect except that a few weeks after their move, Warnie, now ten, was sent off to a boarding school in England. The brothers missed each other terribly, and Jack would count the days until Warnie's next vacation. In 1907 Jack described one of his brother's homecomings: "Hoora! Warnie comes home this morning. I am lying in bed waiting for him and thinking of him, before I know where I am I hear his boots pounding on the stairs, he comes into my room, we shake hands and begin to talk."

Even though he was by himself during the school terms, Jack found plenty to do. He set up a playroom for himself and Warnie in an attic, and his parents had a small table made for him to write on. In "the little end room," as the boys called their playroom, they kept their toys and games and books.

Jack loved knights in armor and the language of medieval times, and he read all he could about the Middle Ages. One source was *Sir Nigel,* a book by Sir Arthur Conan Doyle (the author of the Sherlock Holmes mysteries), serialized in *The Strand* magazine. Another was Shakespeare's plays, which he relished for their poetry. Some of them he had read as early as age eight.

Jack also loved the Beatrix Potter books, such as *Peter Rabbit,* with their "dressed animals" so delightfully like real rabbits and cats and mice and yet like people, too. The stories Jack wrote in "the little end room" show the pleasure he took in creating characters with combined animal and human qualities. Sir Peter Mouse, a fearless fighter against the Cats, was important in the early history of Animal-Land.

Interestingly, there is no hint of Jack's vivid nightmares in the stories he wrote as a boy. The stories are fantasy, in that most of the characters he invented were "dressed animals," but the tone of the writing is matter-of-fact and humorous.

The stories that Jack and Warnie wrote and illustrated in their private room were set in an imaginary world. This world, called Boxen, combined Animal-Land, Jack's realm of talking animals, with India, his brother's domain of steamships and railways. Boxen was not just a backdrop for the stories; the boys were fascinated with the place itself. They drew maps of Boxen and wrote histories of it. While Warnie was away at school, Jack sent him letters about the latest developments in their imaginary world:

> My dear Warnie, I am sorry that I did not write to you before. At present Boxen is SLIGHTLY (?) convulsed. . . . King Bunny is a prisoner. The colonists (who are of course the war party) are in a bad way; they dare scarcely leave their houses because of the mobs. In Tararo the Prussians and Boxonians are at fearful odds against each other and the natives. Such was the state of affairs recently: but the able General Quicksteppe is taking steps to rescue King Bunny. (The news somewhat pacified the rioters).

But Jack's main occupation at Little Lea, when Warnie was away, was reading. His parents both read a great deal, mainly books that they bought and kept, so the house was overflowing with books. As Jack wrote later in *Surprised by Joy,*

> There were books in the study, books in the drawing room, books in the cloakroom, books (two deep) in the great bookcase on the landing, books in a bedroom, books piled as high as my shoulder in the

Among those pictured here at Little Lea are
Mrs. Lewis (back right), Warnie (front left),
Jack (next to Warnie), and Mr. Lewis (front right).

cistern attic . . . books readable and unreadable, books
suitable for a child and books most emphatically not.
Nothing was forbidden me. In the seemingly endless
rainy afternoons I took volume after volume from
the shelves.

So at a young age, Jack began reading all kinds of books. He
read for companionship, for entertainment, for information about
the world. And his hungry and open-minded approach to reading
would last all his life.

One of Jack's favorite authors when he was a boy was
E. Nesbit, author of *Five Children and It, The Phoenix and the Carpet,*
and *The Story of the Amulet.* These books were about a family of
middle-class children whose everyday lives were not so different
from Jack's. But in the midst of their daily routines there was always

the possibility of thrilling adventures: being granted magic wishes, seeing a mythical creature come to life, traveling to the ancient past. "I think I have learned a lot from her about how to write stories of this kind," wrote Jack years later, to a fan of both Nesbit's books and his own.

Jack loved the outdoors as much as he loved reading. When Warnie was home and the weather was fair, Jack and his brother would jump on their bicycles and explore the meadows, hills, and wooded glens of County Down. In those days, as Warren described it long afterward, the country around Belfast was "the empty sky, the unspoilt hills, the white silent roads on which you could hear the rattle of a farm cart half a mile away."

From up in the green Holywood Hills behind the house, Jack saw a scene of natural beauty that fired his imagination. He liked to gaze at the steep, rocky Mourne Mountains to the southeast and imagine that "any moment a giant might raise his head over the next ridge."

Besides beautiful scenery, the place where Jack grew up was also rich in history. Castles, reminders of medieval times, dotted the landscape. And dolmens (huge standing stones) and ancient grass-covered earthworks (fortifications) were evidence of an even deeper history, reaching back thousands of years to the age of Druids (priests of the ancient Celts). One such circular rampart near Belfast was known as the Giant's Ring.

The front windows of Little Lea looked out over Belfast Lough (a narrow bay). The boys had a good view of the ships, and they were as interested in them as ever. This interest carried over into Boxen, where Animal-Land (Jack's half) and India (Warnie's), were islands, and ships figured in several of the Boxonian adventures.

On the far side of the Lough was the long, low line of the Antrim mountains; Jack later described "the interminable summer sunsets behind the blue ridges, and the rooks flying home." Animal-Land, too, had "numerous" mountains, as young Jack explained in "The Geography of Animal-Land."

When Jack was growing up, his extraordinary imagination and writing skills did not seem to be influenced by Christian beliefs. The Lewis family attended church at St. Mark's, Dundela, where Jack had been baptized by his Grandfather Hamilton. St. Mark's belonged to the Church of Ireland (a Protestant church similar to the American Episcopal Church). Jack was taught to say his prayers, and he went to church on Sunday with his family. But he took no particular interest in religion.

In Belfast, religion was bitterly entangled with politics. Ireland was still one country then, and the "troubles" of recent times were in the future. But the Protestant majority in the north of Ireland were terrified that the oppressed Catholic majority in the south would rise up against British rule and take over the country. These rumors of rebellion seeped into Boxen, where one of the earliest recorded events of Mouse-land is the uprising of the Cosy Tribe against the Blue-Bottle tribe. The Cats rebelled more than once.

The adults who visited the Lewises talked about Irish politics all the time, and Jack and Warnie spent many boring hours as captive audience to these discussions. However, Jack turned the grownups' talk into entertainment in the Boxen stories. His "dressed animals" spend most of their time scheming, suspecting schemes, taking revenge, forging and breaking alliances, and making pompous speeches. A man addressing Parliament might be boring, but a *frog* — in starched shirt, tie, vest, coat, and trousers — addressing

Parliament was great fun.

Besides the "interesting carictars" he made up, Jack loved to describe the ones he knew in real life. When he was nine, he began work on a book titled *My Life*. "Papy of course is the master of the house," he wrote about his father, "and a man in whom you can see strong Lewis features, bad temper, very sensible, nice wen not in a temper. Mamy is like most middle-aged ladys, stout, brown hair, spectaciles, knitting her chief industry, etc. etc. I am like most boys of 9 and I am like Papy, bad temper, thick lips, thin and generally weraing a jersey."

Long afterward, in *Surprised by Joy*, Jack wrote a different description of his parents. His father was "sentimental, passionate, and rhetorical, easily moved both to anger and to tenderness," a man "who had not much of the talent for happiness," while his mother "had the talent for happiness in a high degree." It was his mother, not his father, whom he wanted to resemble. "From my earliest years I was aware of the vivid contrast between my mother's cheerful and tranquil affection and the ups and downs of my father's emotional life, and this bred in me long before I was old enough to give it a name a certain distrust or dislike of emotion as something uncomfortable and embarrassing and even dangerous."

Only two months after Jack sketched his parents in "My Life," tragedy fell upon the Lewises. For Jack, it was a disaster so great that he compared it to the sinking of the fabled continent of Atlantis.

Warnie (left) and Jack (right), both looking posed and stiff
in a portrait taken with their father in 1910

CHAPTER 2

JACK LEAVES HOME

ONE NIGHT EARLY IN 1908, when he was nine, Jack became aware that something was wrong in the Lewis household. "I was ill and crying both with headache and toothache and distressed because my mother did not come to me. That was because she was ill too; and what was odd was that there were several doctors in her room, and voices and comings and goings all over the house and doors shutting and opening. It seemed to last for hours. And then my father, in tears, came into my room and began to try to convey to my terrified mind things it had never conceived before."

In February 1908, Flora Lewis had surgery for cancer. She lingered on for several months, while Jack prayed for his mother to get well. When she died on August 23, her husband's birthday, Jack prayed for a miracle to bring her back to life. But he prayed as if he were asking a magician to pull a rabbit out of a hat, and he was not surprised that it didn't work.

Jack and Warnie were left with their father, who was not able to comfort his sons. Even before his wife's illness, Albert Lewis had sometimes been gloomy and bad-tempered. Now he was under great emotional strain, for in the same year that his wife died, his father and one of his brothers also died.

Jack and Warnie were not able to comfort their father, either. "The sight of adult misery and adult terror," observed Jack years afterward in his autobiography, "has an effect on children which is merely paralyzing and alienating." In their own misery, wanting their one remaining parent to be especially calm and reassuring, the boys took their father's outbursts of anger hard. "We drew daily closer together . . . two frightened urchins huddled for warmth in a bleak world."

The world was about to become even bleaker for Jack. Before Flora Lewis died, she and Albert had decided that Jack would go away to school with Warnie in September. Warnie had already attended Wynyard, a small school of about twenty pupils in Watford, Hertford (north of London), for three years. He didn't like it, but in those days young boys were not expected to like school at first.

Albert Lewis shed tears as he saw his two sons off on the ferry. He knew he would be lonely without them, but he geniunely thought it was best for them to go to boarding school in England. In middle-class families like the Lewises, many parents sent children even younger than Jack away to school. It was thought that this was the only way for a boy to get a really sound education.

Dressed in uncomfortable school clothes — a stiff Eton collar and tie, scratchy wool jacket and knickers, and tight boots — Jack and Warnie took the ferry from Belfast across the Irish Sea to Liverpool, England. Jack had never even been to day school before. His mother had died only two weeks ago, and now he was losing

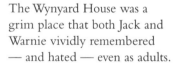

The Wynyard House was a grim place that both Jack and Warnie vividly remembered — and hated — even as adults.

not only her but his home. During the train ride from Liverpool to Watford, Jack concluded that England was flat and ugly. He was homesick for the hills and seacoast of Northern Ireland even before he set eyes on the pair of ugly yellow-brick buildings that were Wynyard School.

If the flat landscape and ugly buildings had been the only problems, Jack could have gotten over his homesickness. If Wynyard had been a good school, with even one adult to give Jack a father's or mother's affection, he might have been happy there. But Wynyard was not a good school, or even an average school. It was a nightmare of a school, with "disgusting food," "stinking sanitation,"

Jack (left) and Warnie — friends as well as brothers — out in the Irish
countryside they loved so much. This photo was taken in 1908,
the year that Jack joined Warnie at Wynyard.

"cold beds," and almost no teaching.

Mr. Lewis knew that Wynyard School used to have a decent reputation; he did not know that it had been going steadily downhill. And of course he had no idea that the Reverend Robert Capron, the headmaster, had been threatened with legal action for mistreating a pupil a few years earlier. Despite this warning, Capron still beat the boys unmercifully for the slightest offense, or no offense at all. Being completely under the power of such a brutal tyrant left Jack with an emotional scar for the rest of his life.

Jack and Warnie learned almost nothing at Wynyard, and it may have been here that Jack developed his lifelong block against mathematics. Most of the schoolwork consisted of "a shoreless ocean of arithmetic" — the boys were ordered to spend senseless hours working one problem after another, with almost no help. They also did not learn to play sports, because there was no playing

Watercolour drawing of the little master, by
C. S. Lewis, rediscovered 1920, with the preceding

1907-8 (?)

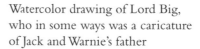

Watercolor drawing of Lord Big,
who in some ways was a caricature
of Jack and Warnie's father

field — only a flinty yard — and no organized games.

The one thing Jack did learn, in his two unhappy years at Wynyard, was to take his religion seriously. On Sundays the boys attended the local Anglican church (similar to the Church of Ireland). For the first time, Jack listened closely to the hymns and readings and sermons and thought about how their meaning applied to him. He also discussed religious questions with the other boys.

Unfortunately, paying attention to religion mainly made Jack aware of his failings, and he became terrified of going to hell. "I feared for my soul; especially on certain blazing moonlit nights in that curtainless dormitory — how the sound of other boys breathing in their sleep comes back! . . . I began seriously to pray and to read my Bible and to attempt to obey my conscience."

Jack and Warnie lived for the holidays, the bright spots of the year when they came home to "civilization," as they called it. One of their favorite pastimes was still writing stories about Boxen, their fantasy world. Sir John Big, the frog, was now Lord Chancellor to King Benjamin Bunny VI, and quite a political power in Animal-Land. Jack admitted later that Lord Big — "immense in size, resonant of voice, chivalrous (he was the hero of innumerable duels), stormy, eloquent, and impulsive" — was an exaggerated picture of their father as the boys saw him at that time. One of Jack's best drawings of Lord Big even has the perspective — from below, looking up — of an adult seen from a child's point of view.

Warnie escaped Wynyard in September 1909, when he was sent to Malvern College (equivalent to a high school), in Great Malvern, Worcestershire. But Jack, too young for Malvern, was stuck in "concentration camp," as he later called Wynyard School. Finally, in 1910, there were too few pupils to keep the school open. Not long afterward, the Reverend Robert Capron was certified as insane.

Jack spent the fall term of 1910 at home in Belfast, attending Campbell College. Then Mr. Lewis decided to send him to Cherbourg Preparatory School in Great Malvern. This town was a health resort up in the beautiful hills of Worcestershire, a welcome change for Jack from the flat, dreary land around Wynyard School.

Now that they were attending schools in the same town, Jack and Warnie made their six trips a year back and forth to school together. Together they enjoyed reading on the train, eating out by themselves, and arriving at school at the very last minute. The brothers were closer friends than ever.

Albert Lewis longed to be close to his sons, too. He tried to make up for the loss of their mother. When the boys were home, he showered them with attention, treating them to special events such as vaudeville shows and musical comedies in Belfast. He expected them to share their private letters and papers with him, and he

An illustrated page from the Boxen manuscripts. Jack's fascination with "dressed animals" is clear — as is his sense of humor.

wanted to know all about their lives at school.

However, Jack and Warnie, twelve and fourteen, were now separated from their father by their mother's death and their years away at school in England. They were no longer frightened by his outbursts of temper, but they found them ridiculous. As young adolescents, they felt naturally superior to their middle-aged father. They regarded their private hideout, "the little end room," as their real home in Belfast.

Jack wrote new and more sophisticated Boxen adventures. The two nations of Boxen, Animal-Land and India, were united under a joint Parliament. But the actual power in the government of Boxen was held by Lord Big, who now had the title of Little-Master. He was also the guardian and advisor of the two young rulers, King Benjamin Bunny VII (son of Benjamin VI) of Animal-Land and Hawki V, the Rajah of India.

In the Boxen stories, Lord Big acts like an annoying parent. Repeatedly he questions the young kings about where they have been, tells them when to go to bed, and reminds them to wear hats and coats. Bunny and Hawki run wild whenever they get a chance.

Another prominent character in Boxen was Second Lieutenant James Bar, a "bumptious little bear" of a "lax, humorous and somewhat loose character." On his first appearance Jack described him with obvious pleasure: "His fur was of a rich hock-brown color, & well oiled on the top of his round head. His expression was humurous, self satisfied, & intelligent." James Bar, like the young kings, was always testing the patience of Lord Big.

These stories that Jack wrote during the years when he was at Cherbourg and Warnie was at Malvern were to be the last of Boxen for many years.

✤ ✤ ✤ ✤

After his two wasted years at Wynyard, Jack flourished at Cherbourg, a real school. He made rapid progress in his studies. At the age of twelve, he was small and unathletic, but he entertained the other boys by telling stories and clowning.

At Cherbourg, at least in the beginning, Jack enjoyed the motherly care of the school's matron, Miss Cowie. "We all loved her," wrote Jack later — "I, the orphan, especially." Unfortunately, Miss Cowie left the school not long after Jack came to Cherbourg.

Meanwhile, Jack was wrestling more than ever with the problems of faith. He suffered agonies of guilt over his sins, both real and imagined. He tried to pray, but he was so self-conscious that all he could think about was whether he was praying the right way.

In studying history and Latin, Jack learned about the religions of ancient Rome and Greece, which no one believed in anymore. He began to think that the Christian religion was also a collection of outdated myths. Why should he believe in those particular myths just because he was told to? Jack was vastly relieved when he concluded that he didn't have to fear going to hell, because there was no such place. And that he didn't have to struggle to pray, because there was no one to pray to.

Soon after he came to Cherbourg, Jack began to experience new pangs of a feeling he called "Joy." He had first felt it as a younger boy, standing in the garden beside a flowering currant bush on a summer day. This moment in the garden made him remember a moment years before when his brother had come into the nursery with a toy garden, made of moss and twigs and flowers, in a biscuit-tin lid.

Standing by the currant bush and remembering the toy garden, Jack had felt, for a split second, an almost unbearable longing. And the longing seemed to be for something beyond his reach — as it was beyond his reach to be a child in the nursery again, gazing at his brother's beautiful toy garden.

The whole experience was over in a split second, but it made a deep impression on Jack. Although there had been a painful sense of loss in the feeling, it was piercingly sweet, and it seemed to be about something very important. Jack yearned to feel the longing itself again.

As a younger boy, Jack hadn't made any connection between "Joy" and the Christian religion. Now that he was an adolescent, such a connection was the furthest thing from his mind. Instead, it was Northern European mythology that brought back the transporting desire. Catching sight of a picture of Siegfried, the warrior

Hallway in Malvern College

hero of the Germanic epic the *Nibelungenlied,* he was seized with longing: "Pure 'Northernness' engulfed me: a vision of huge, clear spaces hanging above the Atlantic in the endless twilight of Northern summer, remoteness, severity."

The sight of the picture and the yearning Jack felt reminded him of something he had read a long time ago: a poem about the death of the Norse Sun-god, Balder. Eager to feel "Joy" again, Jack proceeded to read everything he could lay his hands on about Northern European myths. He began to listen with rapturous pleasure to the dramatic music of Richard Wagner's operas about those myths. And he started to write his own heroic poem on the legend of the Nibelungen, the dwarfs whose treasure and magic ring were stolen by Siegfried.

Once reminded of that piercing, yearning feeling he called

"Joy," Jack also discovered that nature could produce the feeling. Now he paid special attention to the mood of a steep hillside covered with firs, or a sunny glade in the woods, or a dry, rocky valley. As he put it years later, reading "of enchanted woods . . . makes all real woods a little enchanted."

✢ ✢ ✢ ✢

In the spring of 1913, when he was fourteen, Jack won a scholarship to Malvern College. This achievement shows how well he had done at Cherbourg Preparatory School, because he was sick in bed, with a high temperature, when he took the scholarship examination. Now Jack looked forward eagerly to further successes at Malvern.

However, Warnie would not be riding the train to Great Malvern with Jack anymore. Beginning in September of 1913, Warnie was to be tutored privately for the entrance examinations to Sandhurst, a military academy. Warnie had not done well in his studies at Malvern, but he had enjoyed himself socially. So Jack expected to love the school just as much as his brother had.

But for Jack, Malvern College was not the delight that Warnie had promised. To be accepted socially, a boy had to be good at sports and make a good impression on the ruling clique of older boys. Books and music, Jack's two passions, didn't seem to matter at Malvern. Because of his natural clumsiness, Jack was not athletic, and he wasn't even interested in watching sports. And he didn't see why he should try to please the older boys if he didn't respect them.

The social elite of the senior boys were also the prefects, or student monitors — the official power structure in the school. They

Lewis's dormitory at Malvern College

could punish a younger boy just because they felt like it.

But Jack didn't mind the physical punishment as much as the "fagging system." This custom, common in boys' schools of the time, allowed the prefects to order any younger boy to do chores. Jack was often made to shine shoes between breakfast and the beginning of the school day, when he was supposed to be preparing translations for class. What with the never-ending chores that the older boys loaded onto Jack, the demanding schoolwork, and the required sports, Jack was exhausted most of the time.

Jack's unhappiness with Malvern was one of the rare causes of difference between him and his brother. Warnie thought that his brother should try harder to fit in, but Jack had more spirit than that. He knew he was brighter and better-read than most of the other students in the school, including the prefects. Probably the older boys saw this attitude in his face. Also, Jack had a gift for mimicking and for inventing nicknames, and it must have gotten back to the prefects that he called them names like "Fribble" and "Porridge" and "Blugg or Glubb."

Understandably, Jack did not want to emulate any of the bullying senior boys. Instead, he chose as his role model an adult he and the rest of his class admired: his teacher. Schoolmaster Harry Wakelyn Smith demanded hard work from his students, but unlike the prefects, he was courteous and fair. He gave each boy individual attention and encouragement. Best of all, he shared Jack's passion for poetry. He read poems aloud to the class, Jack remembered, so that "every verse he read turned into music on his lips." Although Smith showed no favoritism toward Jack, all the boys knew that he and Jack appreciated the poetry at a depth that no one else understood.

From the time he was very young, poetry had been an important part of Jack's intense inner life. Now his inner world — at this time, the universe of Norse mythology — seemed "incomparably more important than anything else in my experience."

In his precious spare time, Jack would sneak off to the school library, the one place where a junior boy was safe from fagging. There he read more mythology and more poetry, including the work of John Milton and William Butler Yeats and a collection of Old Norse mythological poems. Transported by his reading, Jack escaped from the "sordid, hopeless weariness" of school to lands of gods and heroes.

Writing was also an escape, although Jack no longer wrote stories about Boxen. Now he wrote about the Northern myths in a long tragic poem titled *Loki Bound*. Loki, the troublemaker among the gods in Norse mythology, was in Jack's poem a righteous rebel.

As Jack noted in his autobiography, in *Loki Bound* he expressed both his rebelliousness against the ruling senior boys at Malvern and his rebelliousness against the Christian doctrines he had been taught. "I maintained that God did not exist. I was also very angry with God for not existing. I was equally angry with Him for creating a world."

Years after Jack's experience at Malvern, Donald Hardman, who had shared a study with Jack there, was puzzled to learn how unhappy Jack had been at their school. Hardman remembered many happy times they had had together, especially when Jack would tell stories and mimic people during Sunday walks. Actually, Jack was so miserable at Malvern that he wrote to his father several times, begging him to let him leave.

In March 1914, Jack wrote his father an especially desperate letter. Albert Lewis finally consented to let Jack quit Malvern, provided he finished out the school year through July. In September, Mr. Lewis decided, Jack would begin studying with William T. Kirkpatrick, the same private tutor who had prepared Warnie so well for the entrance examinations to the Royal Military Academy at Sandhurst.

Jack was so happy about this decision that he felt he could tolerate one more term at Malvern. Home in Belfast for the April holiday, Jack happened to visit a neighbor boy his brother's age, Arthur Greeves. Jack found Arthur reading a book called *Myths of the Norsemen*. Jack was electrified. He had never told anyone how he felt about "Northernness" — Valkyries and heroes like Siegfried and "huge, clear spaces hanging above the Atlantic in the endless twilight of a Northern summer." He had not even imagined that his immensely important inner life could be shared.

"Do *you* like that?" exclaimed Jack. "Do *you* like that?" asked

Arthur, just as amazed.

Thus began Jack's first close friendship outside his family. The "First Friend," he explained later in *Surprised by Joy,* is the one "who first reveals to you that you are not alone in the world by turning out (beyond hope) to share all your most secret delights. There is nothing to be overcome in making him your friend; he and you join like raindrops on a window." During Jack's final term at Malvern, he began to write Arthur long, eager letters full of ideas about books and music and nature.

At the end of July, Jack happily left Malvern behind and returned home for the summer holidays. In August, England declared war on Germany. World War I, which would slaughter a third of the men of Jack's generation (including many of the prefects of Malvern), had begun. But for now, Jack Lewis was safe from both the misery of boarding school and the horrors of war.

In September 1914, at the age of fifteen, Jack left Little Lea and crossed the Irish Sea to England once more. This time he traveled to Great Bookham, a village in Surrey, south of London. There he would live and study with his tutor, William T. Kirkpatrick.

Train station at Great Bookham where Lewis first met
W.T. Kirkpatrick, his tutor for the next two years

CHAPTER 3

THE GREATEST PLEASURE

AT THE GREAT BOOKHAM TRAIN station, Jack was met by a man "over six feet tall, very shabbily dressed (like a gardener, I thought), lean as a rake, and immensely muscular. His wrinkled face seemed to consist entirely of muscles, so far as it was visible; for he wore mustache and side whiskers with a clean-shaven chin." This was William T. Kirkpatrick, the tutor with whom Jack was to study for the next two-and-a-half years. He would live with Kirkpatrick and his smaller and much more sociable wife at their house, "Gastons."

During the short walk from the train station, through the little village of Great Bookham, Jack got an inkling of his tutor's startling personality. Kirkpatrick had been the headmaster at Albert Lewis's school and his favorite teacher, and Mr. Lewis had talked to his sons a great deal about the Scots educator. With his father's nostalgic stories in mind, Jack had expected to meet a man as openly emotional as his father. In the first few minutes, Jack discovered that Kirkpatrick was nothing of the kind. Also, unlike Mr. Lewis, the tutor was relentlessly logical.

> I said I was surprised at the "scenery" of Surrey; it was much "wilder" than I had expected.
>
> "Stop!" shouted Kirk with a suddenness that made me jump. "What do you mean by wildness and what grounds had you for not expecting it?"

After close questioning, Jack had to admit that he had only the vaguest idea of what he meant by the word "wildness." Besides, he knew nothing about the scenery of Surrey. "Do you not see, then," concluded Kirkpatrick, not unkindly, "that you had no right to have any opinion whatever on the subject?"

Jack, used to idle chitchat with adults like his father or the family friends in Belfast, was taken aback at first. But before long he was thoroughly enjoying matching wits with his tutor. These intellectual fencing matches became his favorite style of conversation.

Kirkpatrick did not discuss religion with his pupil, but Jack knew that he was an atheist. That was fine with Jack. As he would tell Arthur Greeves, he had already decided that he was "quite content to live without beleiving [sic] in a bogey who is prepared to torture me forever and ever if I should fail in coming up to an almost impossible ideal." However, Jack noticed with glee an *illogical* quirk in his tutor: on Sundays, Kirkpatrick indirectly acknowledged the Sabbath by putting on his good suit to work in the garden.

Kirkpatrick's approach to teaching was as surprising as his conversation. The first day of lessons, he started Jack off reading the epics of Homer in Greek — a dialect of Greek that Jack had not

After the horrors of Wynyard and the disappointments of Malvern, Jack was delighted to be set free from boarding school. He was sent to live with the ideal tutor for him, the eccentric W. T. Kirkpatrick, pictured here with his wife.

studied. The tutor simply read a short passage from the *Iliad* out loud, then translated a longer passage, then left Jack with a dictionary to go over the same text by himself.

This "sink or swim" method of teaching would have sunk many students like stones. But Jack loved language, especially poetry. Besides, he was eager to experience the heroic adventures of Greek legend in their original form, and he made rapid progress. In March 1915 Kirkpatrick wrote to Mr. Lewis that his son had "a sort of genius for translating. . . . He is the most brilliant translator of Greek plays I have ever met." He was also struck by "the maturity

Lewis was grateful to Kirkpatrick for his instruction in the intellectual sphere. He owed his success as a student to him. Ink drawings of W. T. Kirkpatrick by C. S. Lewis

and originality of his literary judgments."

For his part, Jack rejoiced in the challenge to his intellect. He was also glad that Kirkpatrick, unlike Albert Lewis, left him alone most of the time, for his tutor enjoyed his solitude as much as Jack did. And Jack loved the quiet rhythm of life with the Kirkpatricks.

Jack described his daily routine in a letter to Arthur in October 1915:

> I am awakened up in the morning by Kirk splashing in his bath, about 20 minutes after which I get up myself and come down. After breakfast & a short

walk we start work on Thucydides — a desperately dull and tedious Greek historian ... and on Homer whom I worship. After quarter of an hour's rest we go on with Tacitus [a Roman historian] till lunch at 1. I am then free till tea at 4:30: of course I am always anxious at this meal to see if Mrs K. is out, for Kirk never takes it. If she is I lounge in an arm chair with my book by the fire, reading over a leisurely and bountiful meal. If she's in, or worse still has "some people" to tea, it means sitting on a right angled chair and sipping a meagrue [meager] allowance of tea and making intelligent remarks about the war, the parish and the shortcomings of everyones servants. At 5, we do Plato [a Greek philosopher] and Horace [a Roman poet], who are both charming, till supper at 7:30, after which comes German and French till about 9. Then I am free to go to bed whenever I like which is usually about 10:20.

As soon as my bed room door is shut I get into my dressing gown, draw up a chair to my table and produce ... note book and pencil. Here I write up my diary for the day, and then turning to the other end of the book devote myself to poetry. . . .

Both Kirkpatrick and Mr. Lewis found it hard to believe that a teenage boy could be happy without any companions his own age. But Jack could do without the kind of "companions" who had made his life miserable at Malvern. Once in a while Kirkpatrick would take on another student for a few weeks, but Jack did not make friends with these boys, whom he considered intruders from

Warren Lewis, Jack's brother, in the uniform
of the Royal Army Service Corps in 1916

the world of boarding school.

As far as Jack was concerned, he had the best of companions.
Jack was now separated from his brother by his unhappiness with
Malvern and by Warnie's new life as a military cadet, but he had
bonded with his "First Friend," Arthur Greeves. Every week, usually in the evening before bed, Jack wrote two letters. One was a
dutiful report to his father; the other was a letter to Arthur, in which
he poured out his true thoughts. Although Jack and Arthur saw
each other only on Jack's vacations in Belfast, through their letters
they were constantly together during the Great Bookham years.

Much as Jack valued Arthur's friendship, he made it clear
that there were limits to what he wanted to share. To Arthur's hints
that he would like to say something "sentimental," Jack answered,
"Feelings ought to be kept for literature and art, where they are
delightful and not intruded into life where they are merely a nuis-
cance." (Ten years after Jack had written his play "The King's Ring,"
spelling was still not his strong point.)

Accordingly, Jack's letters to Arthur were mainly about books
and music. At one point Arthur evidently complained that Jack never discussed anything else with him, and Jack's reply was indignant.

Arthur Greeves in 1910. Jack considered
Arthur, who shared his love of books,
language, and music, one of his best friends.

"What can you have been thinking about when you said 'only'
books, music, etc., just as if these weren't the real things!"

In his free time, Jack read all kinds of books. He loved science-fiction adventures, such as *Journey to the Center of the Earth*
by Jules Verne and *The Time Machine* by H. G. Wells. He discovered
Sir Thomas Malory's fifteenth-century *Morte D'Arthur,* about King
Arthur and the Knights of the Round Table. "It is really the greatest
thing I've ever read," he told Arthur.

If Jack especially liked a book, he read it over and over. One
such favorite, in spite of its Christian theme, was John Milton's epic
poem *Paradise Lost,* with its vivid descriptions of heaven, hell, and
the Garden of Eden. Another was William Morris's fantasy novel
of heroic adventure, *The Well at the World's End.* (The very title of
Morris's book gave Jack a stab of that inexpressibly sweet longing
that he called "Joy.")

Jack also relished the novels of Jane Austen, filled with her
witty observations on middle-class society, and the historical novels
of Sir Walter Scott. Mrs. Kirkpatrick taught him French while Kirkpatrick himself taught him Italian, and soon Jack was fluent enough
to read books in these languages, too.

✤ ✤ ✤ ✤

During the December holidays of 1914, Jack's father had arranged for him to be confirmed at the family church, St. Mark's. In the rite of confirmation, Jack had become a full member of the Church of Ireland. Jack hadn't been able to get up the courage to explain to his father that since he was an atheist, the ceremony would be a complete sham on his part. He later regarded his confirmation as "one of the worst acts of my life," combining cowardice with blasphemy.

With Arthur, however, Jack expressed his opinions freely. "There is absolutely no proof for any [religion]," he wrote. "All religions, that is, all mythologies to give them their proper name are merely man's own invention — Christ as much as Loki." Later, when he wrote his autobiography, Jack would be embarrassed at his pride in his supposed enlightenment, which in retrospect seemed "incredibly crude and silly."

Perhaps one reason Jack valued Arthur's friendship so much was that Arthur seemed undaunted by Jack's sharper intellect and powers of argument. In spite of his best efforts, Jack never managed to talk his friend out of believing in God. In an earlier letter, Jack had noted Arthur's refusal to stay crushed by his crushing logic: "How funny that I always prove everything I want in argument with you but never convince you!" Some years later, Jack noted ruefully about Arthur, "I learned charity from him and failed, for all my efforts, to teach him arrogance in return."

Arthur might have been unconvinced by Jack's arguments against God because he saw a contradiction between Jack's proclaimed atheism and the books he liked the best. On March 7, 1916, Jack announced that he had found a new favorite:

George MacDonald, the writer
who would prove to be an increasing
inspiration to Lewis as he grew older

I have had a great literary experience this week. . . .
The book, to get to the point, is George Macdonald's
"Faerie Romance," *Phantastes,* which I picked up by
hazard on our station bookstall last Saturday. Have you
read it? I suppose not, as if you had, you could not
have helped telling me about it. At any rate, whatever
the book you are reading now, you simply MUST get
this at once.

Jack loved the dreamy romanticism of MacDonald's writing and appreciated his psychological insights, but there was also a
goodness about this author that deeply appealed to him. Since Jack
thought he had rejected Christianity once and for all, he didn't
understand this effect. But later, he would say that MacDonald had
"baptized" his imagination.

Baptism, the Christian ritual in which a person enters the community of the church, uses water to symbolize the cleansing of the soul for new life. The goodness shining through MacDonald's writing had an almost physical effect on Jack. It was like the pleasure he felt when he plunged into the waves at the seashore, or sank up to his neck in a hot bath.

George MacDonald had also written several children's books, Jack would discover, in which Christian ideas were expressed through fantasy. Much later, Jack himself would find such stories a natural way to express his own experience of God.

Another Christian writer who captured Jack's imagination was John Bunyan, the seventeenth-century author of *Pilgrim's Progress*. Bunyan told the story of his development as a Christian as an allegory, in which the surface of the story conceals a deeper meaning. The journey the Pilgrim sets out on stands for his search for God. The heavy pack on the Pilgrim's back stands for the burden of his sins. A giant who locks him up in a dungeon represents the mood of despair that imprisons him. The Celestial City that he reaches at the end of the story represents heaven.

Besides his taste in reading, there are many hints in Jack's letters to Arthur of a longing for the mystical, for "something strange and wonderful that ought to happen." Although Jack Lewis did not believe in God, he couldn't help sensing the presence of the spiritual world, terrible and beautiful at the same time. All you needed to get in touch with it, he felt, was courage.

Meanwhile, although Jack did not care to write to Arthur about such practical matters, how Jack would earn his living was coming clear. Albert Lewis had been disappointed that Warnie had chosen to go into the military, and he hoped that Jack would follow him into the law. But Kirkpatrick wrote Jack's father, "You may

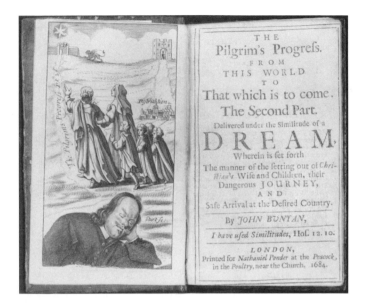

An early edition of *Pilgrim's Progress*, written by John Bunyan in
the seventeenth century

make a writer or a scholar of him, but you'll not make anything else.
You may make up your mind to that." The sensible course seemed
to prepare Jack to teach at a university, and Jack, his father, and his
tutor all agreed that Jack would try for a scholarship at Oxford.

Jack's own ambition, which he did not reveal to his father or
his tutor, was to become a poet. At the end of his evenings, alone in
his bedroom, he wrote poems. "This is the best part of the day of
course," he remarked to Arthur.

For some years now, Jack had been writing to entertain himself, to express himself, to develop his talent — and even to cope
with unhappiness in his outside life. "Whenever you are fed up with
life, start writing," he advised in one of his letters to Arthur. "Ink is
the great cure for all human ills, as I have found out long ago." Two
months later he wrote, "'Work' of this kind, though it worries and

tortures us, tho' we get sick of it and dissatisfied with it and angry, after all it is the greatest pleasure in life — there is nothing like it."

Although Jack thought he was destined to become a poet, his letters to Arthur reveal how much he already knew about the kind of writing — essays and fantasy novels — that would make him famous. The letters themselves were short essays, clear and forceful and witty and personable. In discussing the novels he read, Jack was quick to see how the writers had achieved their effects. For instance, he noticed that touches of "practical, commonsense realism" in fantasy make it all the more convincing.

Jack's letters to Arthur also reveal how easily and vividly he could imagine other times and other ways of looking at the world. In one letter, he responded to Arthur's complaint of not enjoying *Beowulf.* This Anglo-Saxon epic poem tells of a hero who saves a kingdom in the land of the Danes by slaying two grisly monsters.

> If you are to enjoy it, you must forget your previous ideas of what a book should be and try and put yourself back in the position of the people for whom it was first made. When I was reading it I tried to imagine myself as an old Saxon thane [warrior] sitting in my hall of a winter's night, with the wolves & storm outside and the old fellow singing his story.

Besides reading and writing, in his free time between lunch and tea, Jack rambled over the countryside near Great Bookham. He drank in the mood of his natural surroundings. "When you walk through the woods," he wrote Arthur one February day, "every branch is laden like a Christmas tree, and the mass of white arranged in every fantastic shape and grouping on the trees is really wonderful. Don't you love to walk when it is actually snowing? I love to feel the soft, little touches on your face and see the country through a sort of haze."

Jack's first description of Narnia, years later, would be of a snowy woods like this — except that a lamppost would be mysteriously shining in the middle of the woods, and a faun would appear, carrying parcels and an umbrella.

By May 1916, Kirkpatrick felt confident that Jack would be admitted to Oxford with a scholarship in classics. That December, almost finished with his studies in Great Bookham, Jack rode the train to Oxford to take the scholarship examination. And during Christmas vacation, he received notice that he had been accepted, with a scholarship, by University College at Oxford.

Jack spent one more term in Great Bookham, during which Kirkpatrick tried to teach him the basics of mathematics. He did not succeed. However, for the rest of his life Jack was deeply grateful to this tutor, who had taught him the discipline of logical thinking and turned him loose on the classics. Perhaps most important, Kirkpatrick had given him two-and-a-half years in a peaceful, orderly household where his mind could develop at its own pace. "My debt to him is very great," Jack wrote later in his autobiography, "my reverence to this day undiminished."

✤ ✤ ✤ ✤

All the time that Jack was studying and reading and writing and taking walks in the quiet of Surrey, World War I ground on. Warnie (a.k.a. Lieutenant Warren Lewis) had been serving in France since November 1914. Now Jack would soon be on the front lines of the war.

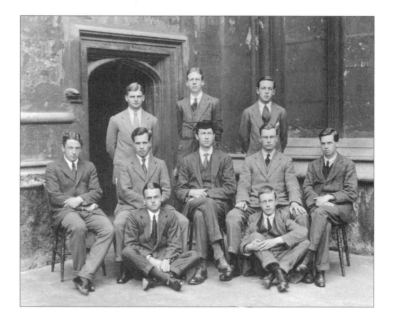

Jack (standing on the right) with fellow class members of
University College in 1917. This class was unusually small because
so many young men were already serving in World War I.

CHAPTER 4

WAR AND RECOVERY

IN 1917 JACK LEWIS was a tall, rather thin young man of eighteen. Pictures taken at that time — of Jack with his father, Jack with his roommate in the officer training program — show him with a reserved expression. But he was not reserved in expressing his feelings for Oxford.

That spring, when Jack enrolled in University College, he wrote glowing descriptions to Arthur. "The place is on the whole absolutely ripping. If only you saw the quad on these moonlit nights with the long shadows lying half across the level, perfect grass and the tangle of spires & towers rising beyond in the dark!"

Set in the picturesque Cotswold Hills west of London, Oxford University had been the center of learning in England for several hundred years. This town of domes and pinnacles and towers reflected the richness of a long span of English history, with some churches dating back to the eleventh century. Jack, with his sensitivity to beautiful settings, his love of past times, and his passion for scholarship, was in paradise here.

Jack was enthusiastic about almost everything in his new environment. He liked his rooms, and he enjoyed rowing on the River Thames. He loved swimming at Parson's Pleasure, a backwater on the River Cherwell, which was a short walk from University College. He reveled in the excellent bookshops of Oxford.

Also, Jack must have enjoyed thinking of all the famous literary men who had attended Oxford through the centuries. The poets John Donne, Joseph Addison, Percy Bysshe Shelley, and Matthew Arnold had walked where Jack was walking now. Jack, of course, was determined to add his own name to the list of famous poets from Oxford.

Besides the poets, many other authors had attended Oxford. William Morris, the author of *The Well at the World's End,* and Andrew Lang, a writer of fairy tales, had been students here. So had Charles Dodgson, better known as Lewis Carroll, author of *Alice in Wonderland.* Although these writers of fantasy were favorites of Jack, he had no thought then of joining *this* list.

Jack did not have long to enjoy Oxford, with its medieval architecture and scholarly traditions. He began his university studies at the end of April 1917; in June, several months after he had turned eighteen, he entered the officer training program at Keble College, Oxford.

Since England was at war, every man over the age of eighteen was required to enlist for military service. Jack could have applied for an exemption from the draft, because his home residence was Ireland rather than England. To his father's distress, Jack refused to take the exemption. He was not at all enthusiastic about the war, but he felt it would be dishonorable not to serve.

Jack (left) with Paddy Moore (right). After Paddy was killed in the war,
Jack became a kind of second son to Paddy's mother.

During his spare time in the officers' training corps, perhaps
spurred on by knowing that he might be killed in the war, Jack
worked hard on a collection of poems. He intended to send it to a
publisher.

By chance, Jack's roommate in the officer training program at
Keble was another man from Ireland, Paddy Moore, "a very decent
sort of man," as Jack described him. Paddy's mother, Janie Moore,
lived in Bristol, in southwest England, but she came to Oxford to
be near her son while he was in training. She was a lively, warm-
hearted, hospitable woman, and she welcomed the company of her
son's friends.

In August, Jack wrote his father that he had spent a week
with Paddy at his mother's lodgings in Oxford. "I like her immensely and thoroughly enjoyed myself." Mrs. Moore was also very taken
with Jack; she later wrote to Albert Lewis about his son, "He is very

Lewis committed himself to fighting in what was believed to be
"the war to end all wars." A battle scene from WWI

charming and most likeable, and won golden opinions from everyone." Paddy's younger sister, Maureen, who was eleven years old,
thought Jack Lewis was "rather slim, but nice looking, talkative."

When Jack had a month's leave in September, he spent most
of it in Bristol with the Moores. Jack's father was hurt that his
son came home to Belfast for only the last week. Jack made vague

excuses about being busy with "adventures" and coming down with a bad cold, but it was clear that he preferred the Moores' company to his father's.

On November 15, Jack heard alarming news: his battalion was ordered to the front lines of the war in France. They were given only two days' leave, not enough time for Jack to go home to Belfast and say good-bye. Jack must have suddenly realized that this might be his very last chance to see his father, and he sent him an urgent telegram: "Have arrived in Bristol on 48 hours leave. Report Southampton Saturday. Can you come Bristol. If so meet at station. Reply Mrs. Moore's address 56 Ravenswood Road Redlands Bristol. Jack."

Jack undoubtedly thought this message was crystal clear, but his father was puzzled. He had no reason to expect that Jack's battalion would be sent to the front anytime soon. Also, Mr. Lewis, like most people in Ireland, didn't know that Southampton was the port from which troops were leaving for the war in France. He wired back: "Don't understand telegram. Please write."

It was impossible for Jack to write and explain in time for his father to meet him in Bristol. He hoped that he might stay in Southampton long enough for his father to visit, but two days later he was on his way to France. By November 29, his nineteenth birthday, Jack was in the trenches.

From there Jack wrote his father reassuring letters like this one:

This is a very quiet part of the line and the dug outs are much more comfortable than one imagines at home. They are very deep, you go down to them by a shaft of about twenty steps; they have wire bunks where a man can sleep quite snugly, and brasiers [pans for holding burning coals] for warmth and cooking. Indeed, the chief discomfort is that they tend to get TOO hot, while the bad air makes one rather headachy. I had quite a pleasant time, and was only once in a situation of unusual danger, owing to a shell falling near the latrines while I was using them.

A letter to Arthur Greeves that Jack wrote from France in December reveals how distant he actually felt from his father. It also reveals how close he felt to Mrs. Moore by then. "Thank you for writing to Mrs. Moore — she appreciated it very much and you may perhaps understand how nice & homely it is for me to know that the two people who matter most to me in the world are in touch." Jack did not feel the kind of strain with his brother that he did with his father, but neither was he as close to Warren as in the old days, before his year at Malvern. And he did not feel free to talk with Warren about his affection for Mrs. Moore.

To Jack's surprise, he liked being in the army much better than he had liked attending Malvern College. While Malvern was supposed to be a sort of boys' paradise, the army was agreed by all to be a hell, and this promoted bonding among the men. "One did not expect to like it," wrote Jack later in *Surprised by Joy.* "Nobody said you ought to like it. Nobody pretended to like it."

Early in 1918, Jack became sick with pyrexia, or "trench fever," and had to spend a few weeks recovering in a Red Cross hospital. When he heard the news, Albert Lewis wrote Jack an anxious letter, and Jack wrote back, asking his father to send him a book. Even in the trenches, Jack had managed to read some novels and poetry. Now he was in a condition he found very pleasant: being

G. K. Chesterton

too sick to work but not too sick to read.

Besides biographies and more novels, Jack read for the first time the essays of the Catholic novelist and critic G. K. Chesterton. He felt an immediate connection with this writer, although he had no idea that Chesterton was a serious Christian. As Jack wrote later, enjoying the joke on himself, "I liked him for his goodness . . . a liking for goodness which had nothing to do with any attempt to be good myself." Jack added, still laughing at his arrogant younger self, "In reading Chesterton, as in reading [George] MacDonald, I did not know what I was letting myself in for. A young man who wishes to remain a sound Atheist cannot be too careful of his reading."

At the end of February, Jack returned to his battalion. Late in March, he sent his father a brief letter, explaining why he had not written before: "We have just come back from a four days tour in the front line during which I had about as many hours' sleep: then when we got back to this [so-called] rest, we spent the whole night digging."

In his autobiography, Jack would describe a soldier's life on the front lines more vividly: "Through the winter, weariness and water were our chief enemies. I have gone to sleep marching and woken again and found myself marching still. One walked in the trenches in thigh gum boots with water above the knee; one remembers the icy stream welling up inside the boot when you punctured it on concealed barbed wire."

Jack never boasted of anything he did during the war; just the opposite. His capture of about sixty Germans he described as discovering "to my great relief that the crowd of field-gray figures who suddenly appeared from nowhere, all had their hands up." Thirty years after the war, he wrote that he did not remember it well. But his graphic description of "the horribly smashed men still moving like half-crushed beetles, the sitting or standing corpses, the landscape of sheer earth without a blade of grass" suggest that he remembered it all too well.

On April 15, during the Battle of Arras in northern France, Second Lieutenant C. S. Lewis was wounded by an exploding artillery shell that killed his sergeant. Jack was taken to a mobile hospital in Étaples, on the coast of Normandy. There it was discovered that

In 1918, Jack posed for a studio portrait with his father. As this photograph suggests, the distance between them was more than physical.

one of his wounds, caused by a piece of shrapnel lodged in his chest, was bad enough to put him out of combat permanently. While Jack was still in the hospital in France, Warren (camped near Doullens) heard that his brother had been wounded. Borrowing a bicycle, he frantically pedaled the fifty miles to Étaples. Warren was greatly relieved to find Jack sitting up in bed and talking cheerfully.

Meanwhile, Paddy Moore had been reported missing on March 24. Mrs. Moore was afraid her son was dead, although she would not get official notice of his death until September. In May, as soon as Jack was transferred to a hospital in London, she came to visit him.

Jack had written to his father, asking him to visit, too. "You will be able to come over, will you not, if only for a few days?" Since Albert Lewis had been terribly worried about Jack's safety ever since he had enlisted, it seems incredible that he did not drop everything and rush to his son's bedside. But Albert wrote back explaining that he could not come; he had bronchitis. The truth was more that he was compulsively bound to his work and the familiar routine of his home.

About a month later, Jack asked once more, in a humble and open way. "I know I have often been far from what I should in my relations to you, and have undervalued an affection and a generosity which . . . an experience of 'other people's parents' has shown me in a new light. But, please God, I shall do better in the future. Come and see me. I am homesick, that is the long and short of it."

But still Albert Lewis did not come. The business of his solicitor's office was too urgent to leave, he explained. Jack was puzzled, then deeply hurt and angry. He knew his father was anxious and habit-bound; it was an old joke as well as a complaint between the two brothers. But he could not understand that Albert was actually imprisoned by his fears and compulsions, and a painful rift opened between them. Although Jack would still be financially dependent on his father for the next few years, he would never again look to him for comfort.

Years later, Warren tried to explain his father's refusal to come to see his son, who had just narrowly escaped death. Warren knew it was not for lack of concern or love. "One would have thought it impossible," he wrote, "for any father to resist an appeal of this kind, coming at such a moment. But my father was a very peculiar man in some respects: in none more than in an almost pathological hatred of taking any step which involved a break in the dull routine of his daily existence." Warren might have added that his father struggled with two handicaps that would plague Warren himself: depression and alcoholism.

Meanwhile, Mrs. Moore gave Jack the affection and attention he had been missing for years — since his mother died. In July 1918, at his request, Jack was moved to a hospital in Bristol, near Mrs. Moore's home. That fall, Mrs. Moore received official notice that Paddy had been killed in action several months earlier. In response to a sympathy note from Albert Lewis, she answered, "I just lived my life for my son, and it is very hard to go on now. Of the five boys who came out to us so often at Oxford, Jack is the only one left. . . . Jack has been so good to me. My poor son asked him to look after me if he did not come back. He possesses for a boy of his age such a wonderful power of understanding and sympathy."

Paddy's younger sister, Maureen Moore, had heard Jack and Paddy exchange promises before they left for the war: Each would look after the other's parent if the other was killed. With his sense of honor, Jack would have considered such a promise to a friend a sacred vow. Undoubtedly he would have taken care of Mrs. Moore as much as he could — visiting, writing letters, offering financial help — even if he had disliked her. Since in fact there was a strong bond of affection between them, it seemed natural for Jack to replace Mrs. Moore's lost son and for her to replace his lost mother. In November, when he was out of the hospital (but still convalescing) at a military depot in Eastbourne, Sussex, Mrs. Moore came to stay near the camp to keep him company.

On November 11, 1918, the Armistice was signed — World War I was over. The following January, Jack returned to Oxford to take up his studies again. He had failed the mathematics part of the entrance examination, but because of his military service he was allowed to enroll anyway. Mrs. Moore and Maureen also came to Oxford and moved into rented rooms on Warneford Road, in the nearby village of Headington.

As an undergraduate student at Oxford, Jack was required

to live at his college. However, he managed to spend a great deal of time with his adopted family, the Moores. On a typical day he would get up at 7:30, have a bath, and go to chapel. (Undergraduates like Jack were required to attend chapel, whether they were believers or not.) After breakfast in the dining hall, he would study or attend lectures until 1:00 P.M. Then he would ride his bicycle to Mrs. Moore's. There he would have lunch, study, have tea, study, have dinner, study, and finally relax with Mrs. Moore and Maureen until 11:00 P.M. After returning to his rooms at University College, Jack would read or study for a short time before he went to bed.

Besides spending a good part of every day with the Moores, Jack was also paying the Moores' rent out of the living allowance his father sent him. Albert Lewis did not know this, but he did gather that Jack felt responsible for the Moores. He knew that Jack, "an impetuous, kind hearted creature," as he called him in a letter to Warren, was providing Mrs. Moore with money now and then. He worried that Jack's involvement with the Moores would hamper his career at Oxford.

In fact, Jack felt more attached to Mrs. Moore than to his own father. Jack tried to conceal this, and he hardly mentioned her in his letters to his father. But Mr. Lewis sensed the estrangement, although he could not understand the reason.

The year 1918 had been momentous for Jack. He had almost been killed in the war, and he had begun a life with a new family. And he had also come a step closer to realizing a lifelong dream.

In September he wrote Arthur, "The best of news! After keeping my [manuscript] for ages [William] Heinemann [Ltd.] has actually accepted it. . . . You can imagine how pleased I am, and how eagerly I now look at all Heinemann's books and wonder what mine will be like." Jack's book was a collection of poems, "mainly strung around the idea that I mentioned to you before — that nature is wholly diabolical & malevolent and that God, if he exists, is outside of and in opposition to the cosmic arrangements."

At this point, Jack saw no reason to change his mind about two important issues: He thought he had no need for closeness with God, and he was more confident than ever that he was destined to become a poet.

Oxford High Street

CHAPTER 5

MRS. MOORE AND MR. LEWIS

YEARS LATER, AFTER Mrs. Moore had died, Warren wrote in a baffled, outraged tone of his brother's "mysterious self-imposed slavery" to this woman. He wondered how much better Jack's life might have been "if he had never had the crushing misfortune to meet her," given what Jack had "accomplished even under that immense handicap."

But Jack's relationship with Mrs. Moore was really not so mysterious, or even unfortunate. Part of Jack Lewis would always be the child who had lost his mother when he was nine years old. It must have been deeply satisfying to him to be fussed over as if he were Mrs. Moore's son, and to gallantly take care of her as if she were his mother. Jack and Mrs. Moore referred to each other, in fact, as "my adopted mother" and "my adopted son." He called her "Mother" or "Minto" (the name of a candy she liked), and she called him "Boysie" or "Boyboys." In May 1920, after Jack had spent a year at Oxford and was allowed to live off campus, he moved into her rented cottage in Headington.

Jack combined "the life of an Oxford undergraduate with that of a country householder," as he wrote Arthur in 1921 with a touch of pride. In the diary Jack kept between 1922 and 1927, he records grocery shopping, tending chickens, chopping oranges for marmalade, washing dishes, and sawing wood. Jack and Mrs. Moore were happy to live outside Oxford in the country village of Headington. They raised vegetables and kept chickens for the eggs. Besides Mr. Papworth, the dog, they usually had a cat or two. They took walks "through fields and wood, all over styles [stiles, or steps for crossing a wall] made of single old stones — rather Druidical looking," as Jack wrote Arthur.

Without Mrs. Moore, Jack might have lived a completely academic life, withdrawn into an ivory tower. "If it were not for her," he told his friend George Sayer long afterward, "I should know little or nothing about ordinary domestic life as lived by most people." Mrs. Moore "was generous and taught me to be generous, too." Jack and the Moores welcomed a constant stream of visitors — friends and relatives staying overnight, coming to tea or dinner, or just stopping by.

Besides doing household chores and entertaining guests, Jack spent many hours tutoring his "adopted sister," as he called Maureen, in Latin and German. Also, for one reason or another, the Lewis/Moore household often had to find a new place to rent. That meant spending time and energy searching for new lodgings for the three of them and then moving all their possessions — books, furniture, animals.

But Jack was energetic enough, and brilliant enough, to manage both a family life and a student's life. He made rapid progress

Jack, looking relaxed, in a studio portrait from 1919. No one would guess that by this time he was already hectically dividing his time between the Moores' household and Oxford.

toward his goal of becoming a university teacher. In the spring of 1920, he took a First Class degree in Latin and Greek literature; in the summer of 1922, he received a First Class degree in ancient history and philosophy. Meanwhile, he had also won the Chancellor's English Essay Prize.

Jack might have been very happy during these years, except that he was burdened with both guilt and poverty. The 210 pounds a year that his father provided was a generous living allowance for a single student living only in his college rooms. But it was not enough to support a family of three, and Mrs. Moore had hardly any income of her own.

Jack and the Moores were always scrambling to get by, doing a range of odd jobs to supplement their income. They took in "P.G.s" (paying guests), who often turned out to be more irritating than they were worth. Mrs. Moore did some sewing for the neighbors. Jack corrected examination papers for the local Oxford schools; because his arithmetic was so unreliable, Mrs. Moore or

Maureen had to add up the scores for him. In exchange for free violin lessons for Maureen, Jack tutored her teacher in Latin.

But worse than the poverty was the guilt that weighed on Jack's conscience. After all, it was Albert Lewis's money that was really supporting Jack and the Moores — the family that Jack preferred to his own father. Jack felt guilty for accepting money from his father and using it in a way that Mr. Lewis would not approve of, for not feeling close to his father, and for deceiving his father about his adopted family. Albert never came to Oxford, except for one brief stop during a holiday, so it was possible for Jack to keep the truth about his living arrangements from his father. But that did not keep Albert from feeling suspicious, or Jack from feeling guilty.

Jack had frequent headaches, presumably from overwork and stress, and he was haunted by guilty dreams. The weight on Jack's mind must have showed in his face, because his friends during the early years at Oxford thought of him as a serious person.

The strained relations between Jack and his father had been made worse by an open quarrel in the summer of 1919, when Jack and Warren visited Belfast together. During the visit, Albert read some of Jack's papers and accused him (justly) of not telling the truth about his finances. Jack burst out with his own accusation, suppressed for years, that Albert had treated the boys badly during the time of their mother's death. It was a sad example of their mutual misunderstanding: Jack could not make allowances for his father's emotional, moody nature, and Albert could not understand how deeply Jack had been scarred by his mother's death and his father's outbursts of temper at that time.

After the quarrel, Albert was hurt and reproachful. Miserably he admitted to his diary that Jack had one cause of complaint against him, "that I did not visit him while he was in hospital. I should have sacrificed everything to do so." But he did not talk it out with Jack, and they carried on with mutual hurt feelings and resentment and guilt. After a period of strain, Jack resumed writing his usual newsy reports to his father. His dutiful, dreary visits to Belfast were brightened only by the chance to spend time with Arthur Greeves, with whom he was still close.

Although Warren felt much the same way that Jack did about their father, he also felt that his relationship with Jack was strained: his brother's devotion to Mrs. Moore put a distance between them. In August 1922, on leave from the army, Warren visited Jack in Oxford in an attempt to share Jack's new life. A highlight of the visit was the brothers' day trip to their old school, Wynyard, where they had been so miserable after their mother's death. Both Jack and Warren took pleasure in revisiting "the hell of Wynyard" as adults who could leave whenever they chose.

During his visit, Warren stayed at first in a hotel in Oxford. But finally he came to tea at the Moore/Lewis house, meeting Mrs. Moore and Maureen for the first time. Mrs. Moore liked Warren, and he liked her well enough at this point, but he was also jealous of her closeness with Jack.

Warren missed the boyhood intimacy with his brother, and he had not found anything in army life to replace it. When the two visited their father in Belfast in September 1922 (Warren was home on leave), Warren accompanied Jack as far as London on the return trip, just to spend one more day with him. After saying good-bye to his brother, Warren noted in his diary "the depression which I have never outgrown at parting from Jack."

Jack, however, was enjoying a new group of friends at Oxford. In spite of his devotion to his studies and his adopted family, Jack still made time to spend with fellow students. At last he had

Parson's Pleasure

found friends, besides Arthur Greeves, with whom to share writing and discuss books, music, and the meaning of the universe. They went for long walks in the countryside around Oxford or met for tea, talking the whole time in a fever of intellectual excitement.

When the weather was warm, they swam in the men's bathing-place in the river, Parson's Pleasure. "I usually go and bathe before breakfast now," Jack wrote Arthur. "I always swim (on chest) down to a bend, straight towards the sun, see some hills in the distance across the water, then turn and come again to land going on my back and looking up at the willow trees above me. It is a most romantic bathe and rather like William Morris [a reference to the author's *The Well at the World's End*] — as one of his characters would 'wash the night off.'"

Jack loved these swims. Floating in the river under the willows, he could be as light and carefree, for the moment, as he had been in his early days with his mother and Warnie during their summer holidays by the sea.

✢ ✢ ✢ ✢

With his outstanding academic record, Jack hoped to be appointed to a fellowship as a don — a tutor and lecturer — at one of the Oxford colleges. He longed to have a decent income at last, and even more, he longed to be financially independent of his father. But with all the young men looking for jobs after the war, appointments were unusually hard to come by.

Even after Jack, now twenty-four, had earned still another "First" degree in English literature, he had to wait two more years for a permanent appointment. Finally he was offered a fellowship in English Language and Literature at Magdalen (pronounced "Maudlin") College, Oxford, in May 1925. The salary was 500 pounds a year, more than twice what he and Mrs. Moore and Maureen had gotten along on since 1919.

Immediately Jack telegrammed the news to Albert Lewis. Then, with enormous relief, he wrote his father a letter that began, "First, let me thank you from the bottom of my heart for the generous support, extended over six years, which alone has enabled me

Magdalen College at Oxford University

to hang on until this."

In September, Jack had a tolerably comfortable visit with his father for the first time in years. Albert Lewis wrote in his diary afterward, "Very pleasant, not a cloud. Went to the boat with him. The first time I did not pay his passage money. I offered, but he did not want it."

Back at Oxford, Jack moved into his fellow's suite of three rooms at Magdalen College. He kept on living with the Moores, but spent most of his time during the week at the college. Magdalen, with its medieval cloister and chapel and tower, is one of the most beautiful of the colleges at Oxford. Its grounds include the lush green water-meadows just across the Cherwell River, circled by Addison's Walk (named after the poet Joseph Addison). Jack's own sitting room overlooked a deer park under the elms.

"From it I see nothing, not even a gable or spire, to remind

Jack loved
the view from
his big sitting room
in his suite of rooms
at the school.

me I am in a town," Jack wrote his father in October 1925. "I look down on a stretch of level grass which passes into a grove of immemorial forest trees, at present coloured with autumn red. Over this stray the deer."

During the years of striving to launch his academic career and support his adopted family, Jack had not given up his dream of

67

becoming a great poet. He had gotten off to an encouraging start in 1919 with the publication of his book of poems, *Spirits in Bondage*. His fellow students, impressed, called him "the famous Lewis" ("jokingly of course," Jack assured Arthur). But not much notice was taken of *Spirits in Bondage* in literary circles. Jack's poems were traditional in style, and critics were more interested in modern poetry, such as T. S. Eliot's "The Love Song of J. Alfred Prufrock."

Jack's father was disturbed by what he considered the blasphemous ideas expressed by some of the poems in *Spirits in Bondage*. "The God I blaspheme," Jack tried to explain to his father, ". . . is not the God that you or I worship, or any other Christian." Of course Jack was not Christian, and he was not worshiping any sort of God. He was only saying whatever he thought would keep his father happy, as he had for years.

In the time between his return from the war and his appointment to Magdalen, Jack somehow found the time to write poems and submit them to magazines — and almost always get them back with rejection notices. He also managed to seize half an hour here or an hour there to work on a book-length poem he called *Dymer*. Jack often suffered from doubts such as those he wrote about in his diary on February 9, 1923: "On getting into bed I was attacked by a series of gloomy thoughts about professional and literary failure — what Barfield [a student friend] calls 'one of those moments when one is afraid that one may not be a great man after all.'"

Dymer is about a man who begets a monster, who then eventually kills his human father. Jack finally completed this long poem in the spring of 1926 — and this time he did not get a rejection notice. *Dymer* was published in a handsome edition by J. M. Dent & Sons that July. Jack's friends praised the book lavishly, and it received some good reviews. But it sold very few copies.

Even now, when C. S. Lewis is world famous and almost any book with his name on it will sell, *Dymer* is not read much. Most readers would agree with critic Chad Walsh that "almost everything that [Lewis] has said in verse he has said better in prose." Jack himself seemed unaware of his real strength; in a diary entry of 1922 he remarked, "My prose style is really abominable, and between poetry and work I suppose I shall never learn to improve it."

✦ ✦ ✦ ✦

After Jack's appointment to Magdalen in 1925, when he finally became able to support himself and his adopted family, relations between him and his father improved. Since Warren was stationed in China between 1927 and 1930, and couldn't get to Little Lea for visits, Jack tried to spend longer vacations with his father. The time Jack spent with Albert was never exactly relaxed, and Jack never felt free to be honest with him about his relationship with Mrs. Moore. But at least the worst of the strain was gone.

During visits to Little Lea in 1927 and 1928, Jack spent hours in his old play room, "the little end room," poring over the Boxen pictures and stories. Reliving this happy part of his childhood, Jack began the *Encyclopedia Boxoniana*. This mock-scholarly work summarized "all that can be known of Boxen and the Boxonian world from the documentary sources alone; the documents including, besides Texts proper, the various Maps, Plans, and Pictures," as Jack introduced it in his stuffiest tone. He wrote to Warren, "It is hard to resist the conviction that one is dealing with a sort of reality. At least so it seems to me, alone in the little end room."

In July 1929, Albert Lewis began to suffer severe abdominal pains. Jack came again to Belfast and spent several weeks there, often staying up all night with his sick father. He was worried and tired, and he missed his brother, the only one who understood how painful it was in some ways to visit their childhood home. "Every room is soaked with the bogeys of childhood," Jack tried to explain to another friend, "the awful 'rows' [arguments] with my father, the awful returnings to school."

Jack wrote Warren about their father's illness, but he urged him not to try to get leave and come home from Shanghai, since it was a journey of several weeks. In September, surgery revealed that Albert Lewis had cancer. Shortly after Albert's surgery, Jack had to send his brother a telegram, which Warren received before Jack's letters telling him that Albert was ill. "Sorry report father died painless twenty fifth September."

Their father's death drew Jack and his brother closer together. They wrote back and forth, trying to take in the fact that their father had died. Jack, as he told Warren, felt a tremendous "pity for the poor old chap and for the life he had led." Perhaps Jack was thinking of his father losing his wife, or his compulsive working and his fear of travel, or his increasing dependence on alcohol. But Jack also remembered his father's love of a joke or a good story, and especially the way he "filled a room." "How hard it was to realize that physically he was not a very big man."

"My father's death," insisted Jack in his autobiography, *Surprised by Joy,* "does not really come into the story I am telling" — the story of his conversion to Christianity. But Jack's struggle to accept and forgive his father, both before and after Albert Lewis's death, seems to have "come into" that story quite a bit. Jack's resistance to forgiving others — and understanding that God forgives — was a major hurdle that he had to overcome before he could draw close to God.

As Jack would later put it in one of his radio talks on Christianity, if you really want to learn how to forgive, don't start by trying to forgive evil strangers, like the Nazis. "One might start with forgiving one's husband or wife, or parents or children . . . for something they have done or said in the last week. That will probably keep us busy for the moment."

Shortly before Albert Lewis's death, Jack underwent a change that would deeply affect his relationships with other people, his teaching career, his writing — his whole life. In 1919, he had come to Oxford as a convinced atheist. In the summer of 1929, greatly against his will ("kicking, struggling, resentful, and darting his eyes in every direction for a chance of escape," as Jack described himself), "I gave in, and admitted that God was God, and knelt and prayed."

Lewis's rooms at Magdalen were behind the three
windows shown at the right end of the middle level.

CHAPTER 6

ON A QUEST

IN 1922, MAUREEN MOORE, along with other girls of her age at school, had been confirmed in the Anglican Church. Jack Lewis, then twenty-four, had dutifully attended the ceremony. "I don't know why I found it very uncomfortable — gave me a sort of suffocating feeling and nervous," he wrote in his diary. The ceremony must have stirred up painful, guilty feelings about his own confirmation in Belfast several years earlier. Jack had continued to hide his true beliefs from his father since then, letting Albert Lewis think — until the day he died — that his son was a regular churchgoer.

What transformed this Jack into the man who, in the summer of 1929, glumly sank to his knees and prayed? A major influence on him was the friends he met at Oxford, fellow students and teachers who shared his passions for reading, writing, and arguing. One of these Oxford friends was Nevill Coghill, also from Ireland, also a would-be poet. Jack met him in an English literature discussion class in 1923. "I soon had the shock," Jack wrote later, "of discovering that he — clearly the most intelligent and best-informed man in that class — was a Christian."

Owen Barfield, who became one of Jack's best friends, remembered meeting him in 1919, over tea in a mutual friend's college rooms. He was struck by "the level gaze and the eagerness behind the level gaze" of the "shabbily dressed undergraduate who bicycled in from Headington."

Jack would fondly describe Barfield, in his autobiography, as his Second Friend, to distinguish him from his First Friend, Arthur Greeves. The Second Friend is the one who is interested in the same things you are but "disagrees with you about everything." Jack, trained in logical debate by his tutor, Kirkpatrick, was delighted to find a verbal fencing partner as good as Barfield. Night after night they stayed up late, arguing. They took long walks, arguing along the way, in the Cotswold Hills around Oxford.

Fighting hard and fair, without ill feeling, was an ideal that Jack had absorbed from stories of medieval times, such as Malory's *Morte D'Arthur*. Another knightly ideal was the quest, an expedition to perform a heroic feat. In the early days at Oxford, Jack was on a quest to discover the most important thing: the truth about God. Truth, he assumed, was to be found through logical reasoning, the kind of logic he had learned from his tutor, Kirkpatrick. As he followed his quest, Jack gathered around him a band of fellow searchers, including Nevill Coghill and Owen Barfield.

In the 1920s, Jack was mistrustful of feelings that did not seem logical. He did admit to *feeling* that there was something beyond the material world, as he explained in a letter to his father after the death of his old tutor in 1921. Even though Kirkpatrick himself had not believed in life after death, Jack was unable to imagine that

Owen Barfield

Kirkpatrick no longer existed in any way: "I have seen death fairly often and never yet been able to find it anything but extraordinary and rather incredible. The real person is so very real, so obviously living and different from what is left that one cannot believe something has turned into nothing. It is not faith, it is not reason — just a 'feeling.'"

Jack might reject such feelings as irrational, but his friends were coming to a different conclusion. Jack felt alarmed and betrayed in 1923 when Owen Barfield became convinced that physical matter is not necessarily the only reality. Our own imaginations, he argued, are proof of a soul. Another good friend, Cecil Harwood,

Nevill Coghill,
in a photo taken in 1972

was already thinking along these lines.

But Jack was as mistrustful of his imagination as of his feelings. True, his imagination could transport him to Asgard, home of the Norse gods and heroes, or to the court of King Arthur. And through his imagination he had escaped from the dreary life of boarding school and the trenches of World War I. However, Jack was often tempted to use his powerful imagination for self-indulgent daydreams of pleasure or revenge, and this worried him.

Jack's imagination could not only tempt him but also terrify him with glimpses of hell. His dreams, including his nightmares, were still as vivid as when he was a child. In one particularly gruesome dream he recorded in his diary, a scientist had managed to keep a corpse conscious and partly alive. "The horrible thing was sent to us — in a coffin of course — to take care of."

In February 1923, something happened to make Jack even more mistrustful of imagination unleashed. His friend and Mrs. Moore's brother, Dr. John Askins, who had never really recovered from the trauma of World War I, went insane. Mrs. Moore and Jack kept him in their home for two harrowing weeks, until they could get him into a mental hospital. Many nights Jack stayed up, keeping watch over "the Doc" as he raved about going to hell and writhed around on the floor. "The worst thing I had to contend with," wrote Jack in his diary, "was a sort of horrible sympathy with the Doc's yellings and grovellings — a cursed feeling that I could quite easily do it myself."

Before "the Doc" went insane, he had dabbled in realms that also intrigued Jack, such as spiritualism (attempts to communicate with the dead) and psychoanalysis (ideas about personality developed by Sigmund Freud, based on dreams, unconscious memories, and so on). Jack took his friend's mental breakdown as a warning to stay away from "all romantic longings and unearthly speculations."

Jack wrote Arthur Greeves with advice that he was determined to follow himself: "Keep clear of introspection, of brooding, of spiritualism, of everything eccentric. Keep to work and sanity and open air — to the cheerful & the matter of fact side of things. We hold our mental health by a thread: & nothing is worth risking it for."

For Jack, "keeping to the open air" included taking a long walk through the countryside almost every day, either by himself or with Mr. Papworth, the dog, or with a friend. A. K. Hamilton-Jenkin, an Oxford student from Cornwall, was a good companion for a walk, like the one Jack recorded in his diary in November 1922:

After lunch I bicycled to Jenkin's rooms. . . . We

started by the Botley Road and went through Ferry Hinksey. . . . When we got to Thessaly we laid our bikes down in the bracken and walked into the wood. We went further than I have ever been, across three ridges. We were as pleased as two children revelling in the beauty, the secrecy, and the thrill of trespassing.

Jack struggled to sort out all the philosophy that he and his friends studied and read and argued about, and his feelings, and to decide how the two parts of him fit together. Often he felt that he was in an "unholy muddle" about what to believe. It made sense to his mind now that there must be a perfect but impersonal spirit, an "Absolute" (he would not call it "God"), in the universe. This was comfortable; he could think about an eternal "hidden glory" without worrying about having to depend on It or obey It.

Then there were the flashes of sublime longing that Jack called "Joy." He was still seeking "Joy" with all his heart. He would find it, just for an instant, here and there: coming out of the Magdalen College library into an early spring afternoon; looking at the sunset as he rode down the hill on the bus; after a morning walk, reading the Greek philosopher Aristotle. Often he would seek out places where he thought "Joy" might come to him, such as "a thick and silent woods" where he could sit on a mossy boulder.

One of the few poems Jack managed to get published in those years was titled "Joy," an attempt to express these experiences. At the time, Jack made no connection between his logical search for truth and the pang of almost unbearable sweetness. Later in life, he would conclude that "Joy" was a kind of signpost, telling him that something crucial was missing and leading him toward God.

Jack and his Oxford friends began to go on walking tours,

One of Jack's most famous friends: J. R. R. Tolkien, author of
The Lord of the Rings in a photo taken in 1973

staying overnight at inns along the way. In the spring of 1927, Jack wrote to his brother, who had been sent by the army to Shanghai, China, about one of these hiking vacations. Jack loved everything about this adventure on the Berkshire Downs (a countryside of grassy uplands not far south of Oxford). Several of the features of this walk would turn up later in his children's stories about Narnia.

A sight that "overwhelmed" Jack and put him into a "dreamlike state" was the village of Avebury, which the friends walked toward over a "slope full of druidical stones." The village was set in the middle of ancient, grass-covered earthworks and rings of enormous stones, erected by the prehistoric Britons. The next day, Jack and his friends hiked through Savernake Forest, a wood of "nearly all big oaks with broad mossy spaces between them," and over a spur of the hills called "the Giant's Grave." Jack described the delight, after a day's hiking, of "looking down into a rich wooded valley where you see the roofs of a place where you're going to have supper and bed."

Even the occasional arguing and blaming and teasing among the friends was part of the pleasure. In one argument that Jack lost, he was for having lunch in a pub along the way, and against bringing a picnic. He described with glee the moment when Cecil Harwood, who had insisted on packing a lunch, discovered that the butter had melted onto his socks and pajamas.

The most famous of the friends Jack made at Oxford was John Ronald Ruel Tolkien, future author of the fantasy epic *The Lord of the Rings*. Tolkien, who was several years older than Jack, came to Oxford in 1925 as Professor of Anglo-Saxon. In looks, he was the opposite of Jack: thin, pale, and elvish-faced. Jack, who had gained weight rapidly since he left the army, was now heavy and ruddy. Tolkien was also quiet and introspective, while Jack was hearty and sociable; married, with children, while Jack was a bachelor; and Roman Catholic, while Jack was from Protestant Belfast.

However, their mutual love of languages and Northern mythology drew them together. With enthusiasm Jack joined the

Kolbitar, a group Tolkien organized for reading aloud sagas in Old Icelandic. "*You* will be able to imagine what a delight this is to me," Jack wrote Arthur. ". . . The mere name of god or giant catching my eye will sometimes throw me back fifteen years into a wild dream of northern skies and Valkyrie music." Like Nevill Coghill, Tolkien was a practicing Christian, but Jack tolerated this "quirk" for the sake of their common interests.

On Jack's quest for the truth about God, the authors of books were his companions as much as his real friends were. Nevill Coghill had noticed early that "although, at that time, [Jack] was something of a professed atheist, the mythically supernatural things in ancient epic and saga always attracted him. . . . The gods were realities for him in the imaginative world, though he rejected God in his philosophical and practical worlds."

Jack himself began to realize that, "curiously enough," most of his favorite authors — Milton, Spenser, George MacDonald, G. K. Chesterton — were Christians. Arguing with authors as vigorously as he argued with his real friends, Jack covered the margins of his books with questions and comments. One book that struck him especially was Chesterton's *Everlasting Man,* outlining the Christian view of history. It made very good sense to Jack.

In fact, as Jack later joked in *Surprised by Joy,* he thought "that Christianity was very sensible 'apart from its Christianity.'" Perhaps by this he meant that he shrank back from the consequences of believing in Christianity. He feared that if he truly believed that Christ was his Savior, it would change his life.

It was Jack's imagination, rather than the logical argument he was so devoted to, that would lift him over the highest hurdle in his quest. One day, riding from Oxford to Headington on the top of a double-decker bus, Jack felt himself presented with a choice.

"I became aware that I was holding something at bay, or shutting something out. Or, if you like, that I was wearing some stiff clothing, like corsets, or even a suit of armor, as if I were a lobster. . . . I could open the door or keep it shut; I could unbuckle the armor or keep it on. . . . I chose to open, to unbuckle." So, in the summer of 1929, at the age of thirty, Jack "unbuckled" — he let God in.

This was a major breakthrough, but Jack did not yet believe in Christ. And he was still terrified of a personal relationship with God. "You must picture me alone in that room in Magdalen, night after night, feeling, whenever my mind lifted even for a second from my work, the steady, unrelenting approach of Him whom I so earnestly desired not to meet. That which I greatly feared had at last come upon me."

As Owen Barfield observed, Jack felt ethically bound to act on what he believed, however uncomfortable it made him. That fall, Jack began going to morning chapel at the college and to church on Sundays; he also began reading the Bible. He wrote ruefully to Barfield, who had himself become a Christian by now, "Terrible things are happening to me. The 'Spirit' [Jack's term for an impersonal Creator of the universe] . . . is showing an alarming tendency to become much more personal and is taking the offensive, and behaving just like God."

In April 1930, Jack and a group of friends took their annual walking tour in the hills of Exmoor (in southwest England). Jack described a hike over a hill, in thick fog, in a letter to Arthur:

We knew when we had reached the top only by the fact that we could find nothing higher and by the cairn of stones over which the wind was hurrying the fog like smoke from a chimney on a stormy day. The descent, largely guided by compass, was even more exciting: specially the suddenness with which a valley broke upon us — one moment nothing but moor and fog: then ghosts of trees all round us: then a roaring of invisible water beneath, and next moment the sight of the stream itself, the blackness of its pools and the whiteness of its rapids seeming to tear holes . . . in the neutral grey of the mist.

Twenty years later, writing one of his children's books, *The Horse and His Boy,* Jack would use a similar setting for an encounter with God. Toward the end of the story, the boy Shasta is hiking over a mountain pass at night, in the mist. He becomes aware, with terror, that a huge, powerful Presence is walking alongside him, hidden by the fog. But the unseen Presence — Aslan — breathes on Shasta and calms him down. Then he says, "Tell me your sorrows."

The boy pours out his heart. He is an orphan, brought up by a harsh, uncaring foster father. He has just made a hard and dangerous journey from Calormen to Narnia; he is tired and hungry and alone and lost.

Aslan listens. Then he reveals that he has been watching over Shasta and caring for him, unseen, all his life. As Aslan finishes speaking, the mist brightens. And that is when Shasta knows that the night is finally over.

Jack Lewis had felt like an orphan ever since his mother died. He and his earthly father had yearned to be close but had failed. Now Albert Lewis was dead, too. Jack was as terrified of God as Shasta was of the mighty Lion — but he had found the One who could share his sorrows.

Jack with his walking stick in 1938. He loved hiking
the countryside of England and Ireland.

CHAPTER 7

FRIENDS, FAITH, AND STORIES

JACK WAS BEGINNING TO FEEL that in order to approach God, just as in getting to know a human friend, he would have to let go and trust. He hinted at this in a letter to Arthur in July 1930, describing swimming in the river with Owen Barfield. "Here I learned to dive which is a great change in my life and has important (religious) connections." A few years later, in his first book from a Christian point of view, Jack would explain what he had discovered about diving: "The art of diving is not to do anything new but to simply cease doing something. You have only to let yourself go."

Jack's brother, too, was gradually coming around to a Christian point of view. While he was in Shanghai, Warren began going to church. When he came home on leave in April 1930, the spring after Albert Lewis's death, he and Jack attended services together, although neither one had yet become a Christian.

While Warren was home, he and Jack also went to Little

Lea, which was to be sold, for the last time. Together they visited the cemetery in Belfast where their mother and father were buried, and in the garden at Little Lea they buried a trunk full of their old toys. These included the stuffed animals and china figures that had first inspired the boys to make up King Bunny, Lord Big, and other characters of their imaginary world, Boxen.

In an earlier letter to Warren, Jack had explained why there was no point in keeping the Boxen toys. The characters that the toys represented, he said, could live only in the Boxen stories. Jack and Warren saved these manuscripts from "the little end room" and brought them back to Oxford. Together, the brothers would keep Boxen alive in their imaginations.

Jack also brought his brother back to Oxford. Warren would never marry, and from now until the end of Jack's life, he would be a member of Jack's household. There was nothing unusual about this in England at that time, and especially at Oxford University. Bachelorhood was an accepted way of life, and often a comfortable one for men like Warren, who had spent so much time in boys' schools and the military.

Although Jack had made good friends at Oxford, he could not be close to them in the same way that he was close with his brother. Warren was a vital link to Jack's childhood, connecting him to that carefree time before their mother died. They had a whole culture of private jokes and nicknames that called up their shared childhood.

For instance, as boys, the Lewis brothers had begun calling each other "Archpigiebotham" (Warnie) and "Smallpigiebotham" (Jack). These nicknames, with their initials APB and SPB, grew out of their nursemaid Lizzie's threat to smack their "piggiebottoms" when they were misbehaving. Delighted with the silly word, Jack

Warren Lewis, Jack's older brother

and Warren took it for themselves. In their private world, "pigie-botianism" (unusual spelling was one of their shared traits) came to mean a high-spirited, carefree attitude toward life, especially in contrast to their father's anxiety and gloom. Even after they became middle-aged men, Jack and Warren would write letters to each other as "SPB" and "APB."

In inviting his brother to join him and Mrs. Moore and Maureen in a house of their own, Jack was concerned that Warren might find it hard to adjust to family life. And in fact, in the years to come Warren would often be irritated by Mrs. Moore's flighty, bossy, inquisitive ways. By this time in their lives, Warren was generally less easygoing than Jack, and less outgoing. Physically, the brothers were similar. They were both about the same height, ruddy-faced and heavy. Warren was somewhat plumper, however, and he had a small mustache.

The lure of living with his brother in such a cultured and beautiful place as Oxford overcame Warren's qualms about Mrs. Moore. Widely read, intelligent, and witty, Warren fit in well with Jack's friends at Oxford, such as Tolkien. He even joined in the walking tours, and those vacations became some of his most cherished memories.

In 1930, Jack and Warren pooled money from the sale of Little Lea with Mrs. Moore's inheritance from her brother, Dr. Askins, to buy a house called "The Kilns" in Headington Quarry, outside of Oxford. Jack and Mrs. Moore moved in that fall, and Warren joined them permanently when he retired from the army at the end of 1932.

The Kilns, named for the disused brick-kilns on the property, was a rambling, vine-covered brick house with many rooms and several fireplaces. The grounds had eight acres of gardens and woods, and a large pond.

Jack wrote to Arthur Greeves that for the first time he was feeling deeply connected with the land in England, as he had always felt connected with the land in Ireland. "I suppose I have been

The Kilns. This was Jack's first real home since Little Lea, and it would be his home for the rest of his life.

growing into the soil here much more since the move." Jack now had a permanent home, his first real home since Little Lea.

At the Kilns, Jack could refresh himself with a swim in his pond every day, sometimes twice a day. "I wish you could join me," he wrote Arthur, "as I board the punt [a flat-bottomed boat] in the before-breakfast solitude and push out from under the dark shadow of the trees onto the full glare of the open water, usually sending the moor hens and their chicks scudding away into the reeds, half flying and half swimming, with a delicious flurry of silver drops. Then I tie up to the projecting stump in the middle and dive off the stern of the punt."

Besides Jack and Mrs. Moore and Maureen and eventually Warren, the household at the Kilns included a maid or two and Fred Paxford, gardener and handyman. Paxford was a hardwork-

Jack, Maureen, and Mrs. Moore at the beach at Cornwall in 1927. Though he
felt guilt about it, Jack was closer to his "adopted family"
than he was to his father.

ing, dedicated gardener, and he became devoted to Jack and Mrs.
Moore. But it was soon a family joke that he seemed to *enjoy* being
gloomy. For instance, if you said "Good morning" to him, he might
answer that it looked like rain or snow — even hail.

✤ ✤ ✤ ✤

Although Jack was regularly attending church in 1931, he
was still disturbed by parts of Christianity. The idea that Jesus Christ
had sacrificed himself to redeem humanity, or that Christians share
their new life in Christ through communion, seemed as emotional
and dramatic as pagan myths. Of course, Jack loved myths passionately, but he thought he knew that they were not "real." His religion
had to be real.

J. R. R. Tolkien, Jack's friend and colleague at Oxford and a lifelong Christian, shared Jack's passion for the world of myth. But Tolkien was convinced that myth, such as the Norse myth of the death of Balder, or the Greek myth of Psyche and Eros, was not the opposite of fact. These stories were a way of expressing truths *deeper than fact.*

On September 19, 1931, Jack invited Tolkien and another friend, Hugo Dyson, an English professor, to dinner at Magdalen College. After dinner, the three of them strolled along Addison's Walk, under the beech trees, in the still, warm night, talking about myth and Christianity. Not only did the truth in myths come from God, Tolkien declared, but a writer of myths could be doing God's work in the world.

As Tolkien talked, there was a sudden rush of wind out of nowhere, as if to underline the message. The three men held their breath, feeling the importance of the moment.

Tolkien and Dyson came back to Jack's rooms and talked on into the early morning. They persuaded Jack that he needed to use his imagination to understand the Christian story. Later, Jack explained to Arthur that the story of Christ's life as a human being and his sacrifice to redeem the world was a "true myth: a myth working on us in the same way as the others, but with this tremendous difference that it *really happened.*"

The whole evening made a deep impression on Jack. He was now only a small step away from becoming a believing Christian. It was on an outing with his brother on September 28, 1931, that he took the last step.

Warren described the day in his diary, unaware of what was going on in Jack's head. "Today the family paid its long projected visit to Whipsnade Zoo after the usual Kafuffle [the Lewis brothers' word for needless fuss] which seems inseparable from a family outing in our house." It was finally decided that Maureen would drive Mrs. Moore, Mrs. Moore's goddaughter Vera Henry, and the dog, Mr. Papworth, in the car. (It was Jack's car, but he had no mechanical ability, and he had never been able to learn to drive it.)

Jack rode to the zoo in the sidecar of Warren's motorcycle. There was heavy fog when the brothers started for the zoo, but as they drove along the fog gave way to sunshine. It was during this trip, Jack wrote afterward, that he finally became a Christian. He was thirty-two.

Telling of this event in *Surprised by Joy,* Jack seems amused that he was transformed into a Christian under such ordinary, undignified circumstances. Later on, he often said that his worst sin was the sin of pride. No doubt he thought it was a good humbling experience for him to be converted to Christianity in the sidecar of a motorcycle, on the way to the zoo.

Jack did not even discuss faith with his brother on this outing. "When we set out," Jack wrote later, "I did not believe that Jesus Christ is the Son of God, and when we reached the zoo I did." It was not an emotional transition, he tried to explain, or one that he achieved through a great effort of will power. It was more like lying in bed, first sleeping — and then aware of being awake.

Later that year, Jack decided to become a practicing Christian — to publicly accept this religion and to try to live by it. On Christmas Day in 1931, he took communion for the first time since he was a boy. Warren, back in Shanghai, did not know this, but he also took communion for the first time in many years on that Christmas Day.

✢ ✢ ✢ ✢

Becoming a Christian had a remarkable effect on Jack's writing. Only a year before, in August 1930, he had concluded that his efforts to become a great poet were a failure. "From the age of sixteen onwards," he wrote Arthur, "I had one single ambition, from which I never wavered, in the prosecution of which I spent every ounce I could, on wh[ich] I really & deliberately staked my whole contentment, and I recognise myself as having unmistakably failed in it."

Perhaps Jack had to give up his quest for literary success — the kind of success *he* wanted — in order to develop his real gifts as a writer. On a two-week visit to Arthur in Belfast in 1932, Jack wrote the entire manuscript of *The Pilgrim's Regress.* Like John Bunyan in *Pilgrim's Progress,* the allegory that was one of Jack's favorite books, he told the story of his life as a journey toward Christian faith.

At the beginning of *The Pilgrim's Regress,* Jack satirized his first idea of Christianity, which developed during his years at Wynyard, as a creed of guilt and punishment. In his story, the boy John is given "a big card with small print all over it" — the many rules of religion. "Half the rules seemed to forbid things he had never heard of; and the other half forbade things he was doing every day and could not imagine not doing: and the number of rules was so enormous that he felt he could never remember them all."

Confused and tormented by these joyless rules, John one day hears a sweet musical note and a faraway voice calling him, and he thinks he catches a glimpse of a beautiful Island. This tantalizing experience fills him with such an "unbounded sweetness" that nothing else seems important, and finally he sets out to seek the Island.

Along his way, Jack's pilgrim confronts fearsome dangers, such as dragons and giants, and many false leads and temptations to give up his search. The "regress" in Jack's title is a jibe at himself. He saw himself as a pigheaded seeker who followed his quest almost all the way around the world in the wrong direction — and then had to retrace his steps.

Published in 1933, this book was dedicated to Arthur Greeves. *The Pilgrim's Regress* was not especially successful at first, but it was the first public sign of Jack Lewis's calling as a writer of stories. J. R. R. Tolkien liked it very much.

Since the end of 1929, Tolkien had been coming to Jack's college rooms once a week to read him installments of *The Silmarillion*. This was an epic, told originally in poetry, of the myths, legends, and history of an entire world that Tolkien had made up. By the time Jack was finishing *The Pilgrim's Regress,* Tolkien was writing a children's story set in the world of *The Silmarillion*.

In February 1933, Jack wrote Arthur Greeves in great excitement over that children's story, *The Hobbit*. Tolkien was, Jack told Arthur, "the one man absolutely fitted, if fate had allowed, to be a third in our friendship in the old days, for he also grew up on W. Morris and George Macdonald. Reading his fairy tale has been uncanny — it is so exactly like what we [would] both have longed to write (or read) in 1916: so that one feels he is not making it up but merely describing the same world into which all three of us have the entry."

Jack's enthusiasm was very important to Tolkien, as Tolkien later acknowledged: "He was for long my only audience. Only from him did I ever get the idea that my 'stuff' could be more than a private hobby. But for his interest and unceasing eagerness for more I should never have brought [*The Lord of the Rings*] to a conclusion."

Charles Williams in a photo taken in 1935. Williams was the author of such fantasy novels as *All Hallows' Eve, War in Heaven,* and *The Place of the Lion.* In fact, *The Place of the Lion* was the first Williams novel that Jack read, on the recommendation of his friend Nevill Coghill.

As for Jack, it was greatly inspiring that he and Tolkien loved the same kind of stories: fiction based on poetic myth.

Warren began meeting with Jack and Tolkien in 1933, shortly after his retirement from the army. The next year, Warren was inspired to begin writing his own first book, on the age of Louis XIV of France. Soon, two more friends, Hugo Dyson and Dr. Robert E. Havard (Jack and Warren's physician), joined the group. The men were now meeting every Thursday evening to talk about what they were reading and writing. They also met on Tuesday mornings, at a pub called the Eagle and Child, for more casual conversation.

So the core of two writing friends had grown into a whole

group, which Jack named the "Inklings." Tolkien explained the nickname as suggesting "people with vague or half-formed intimations and ideas plus those who dabble in ink." Owen Barfield, now a lawyer in London, came to meetings when he was in town, and so did several former students of Jack's, such as George Sayer. Other friends, including Nevill Coghill from Jack's undergraduate days, also joined the group. After World War II began in 1939, Charles Williams, an editor and a writer of fantasy novels, became a regular Inkling.

Almost every week during the school year, for fifteen years, the Inklings met at Magdalen College. They gathered after dinner, at about eight o'clock, in Jack's high-ceilinged sitting room. They settled into the battered armchairs and the large, shabby sofa in front of the coal fire. There was not much else in the room besides a dining table, where Jack wrote, and bookshelves.

On any particular Thursday evening, there might be only three or four, or there might be as many as eight. After Warren brewed a pot of tea for the group, anyone who was working on a piece of writing could read it aloud and receive frank criticism from the group. Although the friends were all Christian, they were not pious. With Jack setting the tone, they argued, teased each other unmercifully, and roared with laughter.

Jack loved these gatherings, and he felt lucky to be living in a place where he could see good friends all the time. As he put it in a letter to Arthur Greeves in 1935, "Friendship is the greatest of worldly goods. Certainly to me it is the chief happiness of life."

Meanwhile, Jack's academic career blossomed. In 1936 he published *The Allegory of Love,* a study of the love poetry of the Middle Ages. In his self-mocking way, Jack referred to this book as "The Alligator of Love," but it was widely praised.

Jack was also becoming a popular lecturer at Oxford, known for his clear and lively presentations. His students would remember him as a tall, heavy man with a big red face who wore rumpled tweeds. One student described Jack's voice as "rich and strong, laced with some characteristic Ulster [Northern Ireland] touches, particularly with his r's."

Many of the pupils Jack tutored became his friends, and some of them, like George Sayer, later attended Inklings meetings. "There is hardly a year in which I do not make some real friend," Jack had told Arthur Greeves in 1931. The following year he described to Arthur the pleasure he got from seeing a former pupil grow intellectually. "I suppose it is this pleasure," he mused sadly, "which fathers always are hoping to get, and very seldom do get, from their sons."

✛ ✛ ✛ ✛

"Tollers," said Jack to Tolkien in the early days of the Inklings, "there is too little of what we really like in stories. I am afraid we shall have to try and write some ourselves." Jack's first attempt along these lines was the science-fiction novel called *Out of the Silent Planet.*

Since boyhood Jack had loved the science fiction of Jules Verne and H. G. Wells. He had always been fascinated with astronomy, in spite of his block in mathematics. As a boy, Jack had even begun a story titled "To Mars and Back." Now he took off for Mars again, reading *Out of the Silent Planet* to the Inklings, chapter by chapter, as he wrote.

C. S. Lewis's descriptions of the Red Planet are so vivid that even now, after Mars has been explored by robots and mapped in detail, his quite different Mars still seems real. But *Out of the Silent Planet,* published in 1938, is especially remarkable for its combination of science fiction and the Christian point of view. Jack's underlying idea of the solar system was that each planet is protected by an *oyarsa,* or kind of archangel. In this story, the oyarsa assigned to Earth has gone horribly wrong, with the result that our planet is a battleground between good and evil.

Throughout the story, Jack used touches of "practical, commonsense realism" that, as he had long ago noted to Arthur Greeves, make fantasy convincing. For instance, during his stay on Mars, Ransom has a chance to look at the Earth through a device like a telescope. The sight of his home planet, to which he may never return, makes Ransom feel unbearably homesick. He thinks forlornly of his backpack, left behind when he was kidnapped during a walking tour.

One of the readers who wrote Jack to say that she loved *Out of the Silent Planet* was Sister Penelope, an Anglican nun in a convent at Wantage, south of Oxford. She was a highly educated woman with a sharp intelligence, and someone he could talk to about religious experiences and personal difficulties. Through letters, they began a friendship that lasted many years.

Long ago, reading George MacDonald's fantasy novels, Jack had felt his imagination "baptized," in the sense that a baby is baptized before it is aware of what the sacrament means. MacDonald's work gave Jack an idea of the kind of fiction that could be written with a Christian imagination. Then, in his long search for the truth about God, Jack had learned that his own powerful imagination could be used to reinforce his Christian faith.

Now that Jack's creative gifts were truly "baptized," or purified, he could use them without spiraling off into madness. Now, without fear of being destroyed, he could imagine nightmares and beatific visions, angels and devils, heaven and hell. His faith both released him and inspired him to write his best.

Jack at his desk in 1947. At this point he had written several books, including *Out of the Silent Planet,* but he would not finish the first Chronicle of Narnia until 1949.

CHAPTER 8

DEFENDER OF THE FAITH

IN 1939, WORLD WAR II broke out. To Jack, it was like the nightmare of World War I starting up again. He had no doubt that England was right to fight Nazi Germany, but he regarded war as a "ghastly interruption of rational life." Again millions of people would be maimed and slaughtered; again entire landscapes would be blasted.

"My memories of the last war have haunted my dreams for years," Jack wrote his former pupil Alan Bede Griffiths, by then a Roman Catholic monk. ". . . I'm not a pacifist. If its [sic] got to be, its [sic] got to be. But the flesh is weak and selfish and I think death would be much better than to live through another war."

In one way, World War II was very different from World War I: this time, England would be directly attacked. Jack, along with other citizens of Oxford, had to dig a bomb shelter near his house.

Fittingly for this pain-filled time in England's history, Jack was working on a book called *The Problem of Pain*. In it he explained what Christians believe about why there is suffering in the world. It was his first book of apologetics, or defense of Christian beliefs. As he wrote, Jack read *The Problem of Pain* aloud to the Inklings, and he dedicated the book to them.

Jack was over forty, too old to be drafted. But he served in the Home Guard, the part-time soldiers who would fight if German troops attempted to land from the air. His duty, as he described it to Arthur, amounted to spending late nights "mouching about the most depressing and malodorous parts of Oxford with a rifle." He worried about Warren, who as an officer in the reserve was called up in 1939 and sent to France. However, the following summer Warren and many other retired officers were released from active duty and spent the rest of the war in the Home Guard.

In Oxford, Jack and his friends had to keep their houses blacked out at night to prevent enemy aircraft from spotting them and using them as targets. It was tedious to put the blackout curtains up every evening and take them down every morning, but otherwise Jack rather liked the blackouts. He described a frosty, moonlit January night as "very beautiful . . . in Oxford now that there are no lighted windows or street lamps to spoil it."

There were frequent air-raid alerts, although Jack and the Moores soon stopped going to the cold, damp dugout shelters at every warning. Coal was rationed, so wood had to be sawed for heating. And Jack and Mrs. Moore opened their home to children from London, which, unlike Oxford, was being savagely pounded with air raids.

One of these London refugees, Margaret M. Leyland, remembered Jack long afterward as a "kind and sympathetic" man

Inside the Kilns, the home of Lewis, the bedroom in which Lewis died

who never talked down to "us school girls." The Kilns, a country household with its own chickens and fresh vegetables, didn't suffer from wartime food rationing as much as city families. However, Mrs. Moore had become rather stingy in her old age, and she did not allow Margaret and the other refugees as much food as they wanted. But Jack would smuggle extra rations up to their room at night, or sneak the girls out to a fish-and-chips shop. He let Margaret look at the stars through the telescope on his balcony, and he would entertain her and the other girls with stories while they took walks or sat in the garden.

Living with these refugee children must have awakened something in Jack, because he made notes for a children's story. It was to be about two brothers and two sisters who are sent to the country to escape the air raids in London, and stay with an old professor.

☩ ☩ ☩ ☩

During the early years of World War II, it seemed entirely likely that Nazi Germany could defeat England. Germany quickly overran France, and then England was only eighteen miles across the English Channel from Hitler's bombers.

The sense of living in a country under siege by diabolical powers comes out in *The Screwtape Letters.* While Jack was writing this book, he read it to the Inklings on Thursday evenings, much to their enjoyment. He dedicated *Screwtape,* his first really successful book, to J. R. R. Tolkien.

The story is set in England during World War II, but the real war is not between England and Germany — it is between good and evil. In *The Screwtape Letters,* as in Jack's science-fiction novels, humankind is secretly under attack by demons. They work tirelessly to lure human beings into sin, away from God.

Screwtape was (and still is) popular partly because of Jack's down-to-earth way of explaining good and evil. For the human under attack in this story, one of the greatest temptations to sin is daily life with his own mother, "the sharp-tongued old lady at the breakfast table." Simple pleasures like watching a cricket game or drinking cocoa are hateful to devils because they encourage "innocence and humility and self-forgetfulness." A soul entering Heaven feels something like Jack enjoying his bath — "taking off dirtied and uncomfortable clothes and splashing in hot water and giving little grunts of pleasure."

Jack hated war, but not because he believed that killing is

always wrong. In one of a series of radio talks on Christianity that he gave during the war, he summed up what he thought about killing and its connection to his faith: "The idea of the knight — the Christian in arms for the defence of a good cause — is one of the great Christian ideas."

The idea of the medieval knight had caught Jack's imagination early on. As a boy, even after he decided that Christianity was only a human invention, he delighted in tales of King Arthur and the Knights of the Round Table. Now he believed that Christians fighting for England against Hitler's armies should not be ashamed of killing for this good cause. They had a right, in fact, to "something which is the natural accompaniment of courage — a kind of gaiety and wholeheartedness."

The Christian as a valiant knight had already appeared in *The Pilgrim's Regress,* and the image would reappear in his second science-fiction novel, *Perelandra.* In this story, set on the planet Venus, a Christian from Earth plays an important role in the struggle between good and evil. The hero, Ransom, has to fight to the death with a scientist who has been possessed by Satan.

As he worked on *Perelandra,* Jack read chapters of this book, as he did all his writing, to the Inklings. He also wrote letters discussing his writing to Sister Penelope, the nun who had first written to him about *Out of the Silent Planet.* When *Perelandra* was finished, he dedicated it to "Some Ladies at Wantage," meaning Sister Penelope and the other nuns of the Community of St. Mary the Virgin, who appreciated his science fiction.

The Inklings were in fine form these days, entertaining and encouraging each other. "Is any pleasure on earth as great as a circle of Christian friends by a good fire?" Jack asked in a letter to Alan Bede Griffiths. Charles Williams, an editor and novelist whom Jack

Owen Barfield, one of Jack's lifelong friends, in a photo taken in 1983

greatly admired, was a regular at Inklings meetings during this period. On Thursday nights, J. R. R. Tolkien was reading the circle of Christian writers his new epic, *The Lord of the Rings.* Jack, or rather Jack's deep, resonant voice, appeared in Tolkien's story as the booming voice of the character Treebeard.

✤ ✤ ✤ ✤

In 1941, the director of religious broadcasting at the BBC (British Broadcasting Corporation) asked Jack to give a series of radio talks on Christianity. Although he disliked modern inventions and avoided even *listening* to the radio, Jack agreed, because he thought he could reach more people this way. And he had an excellent voice for radio, deep and rich, and a knack for talking in a direct, forceful way that anyone could understand.

When he spoke on the radio, Jack used the imagery of the war that was raging in Europe. "Enemy-occupied territory — that is what this world is. Christianity is the story of how the rightful king has landed, you might say landed in disguise, and is calling us all to take part in a great campaign of sabotage."

Jack was also asked to speak on the Christian faith at Royal Air Force bases. He felt this was the least he could do for the war effort, and he spent his weekends and vacations traveling to RAF bases all over England. At the same time, Jack wasn't sure he was the right person to be preaching to military men. "As far as I can judge they were a complete failure," he wrote Sister Penelope about his first series of talks, which he gave at the RAF base in Abingdon. These talks were probably too much like college lectures to appeal to men going into battle, and they were never as successful as his radio talks.

Jack loved debate, and he loved using his talent for it to defend the Christian cause. However, he did not think for a minute that he had a right to preach because he was *better* than his listeners. Jack thought one of his best qualifications for arguing for Christianity was that he had recently been an arrogant atheist himself.

Perhaps another reason why Jack Lewis could reach people outside the church was that he was not "churchy" himself. "Though I liked clergymen as I liked bears," he would remark in *Surprised by Joy*, "I had as little wish to be in the Church as in the zoo." He attended Sunday services because he felt the Christian discipline was good for him, not because he liked them. Church ceremonies, like any ceremony, made him feel awkward. He hated hymns and organ music, and he preferred to pray by himself.

Jack's radio talks on Christianity were enormously popular. George Sayer, a former student and friend, later remembered being in a pub during the war when one of Jack's talks came on the radio. "You listen to this bloke," shouted the bartender to the soldiers crowding the room. "He's really worth listening to."

Many thousands of listeners agreed, and hundreds of them wrote letters to Jack. He gave another series of radio talks partly to answer their questions, but these talks were even more popular, and piles of mail poured in. Warren, who wrote well and could type (although only with two fingers), began acting as Jack's secretary, using one of Jack's rooms at Magdalen College as an office. He sorted the letters, typed replies from Jack's drafts, and often actually wrote letters for Jack to sign.

Jack hardly ever saved letters from other people, but his own letters give an idea of what people wrote to him about. "One gets funny letters after broadcasting," he wrote Arthur in December 1941, "some from lunatics who sign themselves 'Jehovah' or begin, 'Dear Mr Lewis, I was married at the age of 20 to a man I didn't love' — but many from serious inquirers whom it was a duty to answer fully."

People asked Jack how to deal with low periods in their faith. They asked him if he really thought science was evil, and if communing directly with God wasn't more important than following Christian doctrines. They trusted him with their most personal problems. For the rest of his life, Jack would be a sort of pastoral counselor, through letters, to many people.

Jack's radio talks were published one series at a time, later to be collected under the title *Mere Christianity*. Between the success of his talks and the success of *The Screwtape Letters*, Jack was becoming a celebrity. He was also making money from his books

— money which he immediately gave away to charities. After his years of near-poverty in the 1920s, he had great sympathy for anyone who needed money.

Even though Warren was a great help with the correspondence his brother received, Jack answered so many letters in longhand that he developed severe rheumatism in his right hand. Also, after Maureen married and left the Kilns in 1941, he spent a great deal of time with Mrs. Moore, who was in poor health. As she grew older and sicker, Mrs. Moore became more and more difficult. She quarreled with housekeepers or maids who worked at the Kilns, and she insisted that Jack himself wait on her.

In November 1941 Jack asked Sister Penelope to pray for "the old lady I call my mother and live with . . . — an unbeliever, ill, old, frightened." Two years later he wrote Arthur, "Things are pretty bad here. Minto's [Mrs. Moore's] varicose ulcer gets worse and worse, domestic help harder and harder to come by."

Jack was grieved by the fact that his adopted mother never became a Christian. Worse, she seemed to resent Jack's faith for creating a distance between them. Out of his sadness and frustration, he created a character like her in *The Great Divorce* (published in 1945). Imagining what heaven and hell might be like, Jack described a lost soul who could be Mrs. Moore. She is a mother who will not admit that her love for her son is smothering and selfish. "No one has a right to come between me and my son," she declares. "Not even God."

As if he did not have enough to do, in 1942 Jack agreed to become president of a new society at Oxford, the Socratic Club. This club invited to its weekly meetings two speakers, an atheist and a Christian. Each speaker would present his or her case, and then there would be a general discussion.

The idea of Christians challenging unbelievers to a public debate appealed to many others besides Jack, and during the war years the Socratic Club meetings were crowded. The audience was usually rewarded by hearing Jack vigorously defend the Christian side. Many people who knew Jack remember his courtesy, even in a fierce debate — fitting to his ideal of knightly behavior.

In his scant spare time, Jack wrote book after book. In 1943 he finished the third and last novel in his science-fiction trilogy, *That Hideous Strength*. This story continues Jack's theme of the war between good and evil: the forces of evil take over a university town (rather like Oxford), and they threaten to take over the world. The forces of good, as Jack must have delighted in imagining, include a Scottish philosopher like Jack's old tutor Kirkpatrick, a bear from the Whipsnade Zoo, and the great magician Merlin.

Meanwhile, the Inklings continued to meet. Jack read his manuscripts to the group. Charles Williams read installments of his novel *All Hallows' Eve*. And Warren read chapters of his book on the age of Louis XIV, and was relieved and pleased that the Inklings liked them. Tolkien thought Warren's history "wittily written (as well as learned)."

Toward the end of the war, and afterward as food rationing continued in England, Jack's admirers in the United States sometimes sent him food packages. Then the Inklings would begin their evening meeting with a feast of that fabulous luxury, a real ham.

World War II finally ended on May 9, 1945. For Jack and the other Inklings, rejoicing that the war was over was muted by Charles Williams' sudden death during surgery on May 15. It was a painful loss for Jack, who had considered Williams one of his closest friends. At the same time, as he wrote to Owen Barfield with a sense of wonder, he now found it much easier to believe in life after death. He *felt* Williams' presence, as "a sort of brightness and tingling," even closer now.

✣ ✣ ✣ ✣

By the time the American literary critic Chad Walsh visited him in 1948, Jack Lewis was a well-known figure around Oxford, partly because of the extremely casual way he dressed. Students remember him striding around campus in wrinkled gray-flannel trousers and a worn, brown tweed jacket that was too tight. He often carried a knobbed walking stick and wore an old tweed fisherman's hat, which he lost more than once.

One day during Walsh's visit, as he and Jack were walking through a park, Jack suddenly stopped in front of a bush. A shapeless piece of brown cloth was hanging from a branch. "That looks like my hat," said Jack. Then, trying it on, he exclaimed in a tone of delight, "It *is* my hat!"

After his visit, Walsh commented that photographs of Jack Lewis did not give a good idea of what the man was really like in person. He noted Jack's quick, spontaneous smile. "His most striking trait is the aliveness of his face. His expression changes, lights up, as he talks or listens."

The year before Chad Walsh's visit, Jack had published another book, in his role as a defender of the faith, called *Miracles.* He had been thinking about writing an up-to-date book on this subject for some time. To Jack, real Christianity meant believing in the possibility of the miraculous — "an interference with Nature by supernatural power." *Miracles,* which Jack dedicated to his friend Cecil Harwood and his wife, was a popular success, but some theologians and philosophers were critical of Jack's arguments.

In February 1948, a Roman Catholic philosopher, Elizabeth Anscombe, challenged Jack on his own turf, at a meeting of the Oxford Socratic Club. Anscombe was ruthless and brilliant in her attack on Jack's reasoning about Christianity. Jack's Christian faith was not shaken, but he lost some of his confidence in how much he could accomplish for it through argument.

Maybe at this point Jack remembered something he had written in 1939 to Sister Penelope, in answer to her letter about the first of his science-fiction novels. Most reviewers of *Out of the Silent Planet,* he noted, had entirely missed its connection with Christianity. But their ignorance might actually be a good thing. "Any amount of theology can now be smuggled into people's minds under cover of romance [a story of adventure and heroism] without their knowing it."

Or perhaps Jack reread the notes he had made, several years earlier, for a story about four children named Ann, Martin, Rose, and Peter. They are sent to the country to escape the air raids in London, and they stay with an old professor. Now Jack thought of his goddaughter Lucy, the child of his friend Owen Barfield. In Jack's first children's book, *The Lion, the Witch and the Wardrobe,* a girl named Lucy would discover Narnia.

The wardrobe, hand-carved by Jack's grandfather, that
Jack played in as a child. It would open the door to
fantasy in *The Lion, the Witch and the Wardrobe.*

CHAPTER 9

Escape to Narnia

JACK LEWIS SAW NOTHING wrong with escape. In the mid-1950s, he would vigorously defend J. R. R. Tolkien's fantasy epic *The Lord of the Rings* against critics who had called it "escapism." "What we chiefly escape [in reading this book]," he wrote, "is the illusions of our ordinary life." Or, as he pointed out in a talk on science fiction, who are the people most eager to prevent escapes? Jailers. To Jack, writing fantasy stories was a way to break out of the narrow, cramped, "real" world into the spacious, and just as real, world of the imagination.

In the late 1940s, Jack had a great deal to escape from. World War II was over, but food shortages and rationing continued in England. On a trip to Scotland in 1946 with Jack, Warren wrote excitedly in his diary, "Breakfast showed us the difference it makes to get out of miserable hungry England — real porridge, of which I had almost forgotten the taste, plenty of butter, edible sausages, toast,

Jack (left) and Warren
in Ireland in 1949. The two
brothers remained close
all of their lives.

marmalade, coffee!"

There were worse hardships than food shortages. Jack's brother suffered bouts of depression, and every so often his depression would lead to a drinking binge. In the summer of 1947, on a holiday by himself in Ireland, Warren drank so heavily that he became seriously ill and ended up in a hospital in Drogheda, north of Dublin. Jack rushed over from Oxford and stayed with his brother until he was well enough to leave the hospital.

Overwhelmed with gloom and anxiety and guilt, Warren wrote in his diary, "I was struck with the haunting fear that is so often with me — suppose J[ack] were to die before I did? And a sheer wave of animal panic spread over me at the prospect of the empty years."

At the same time, Mrs. Moore was becoming more and more difficult to live with. The varicose ulcers in her legs now kept her bedridden in her upstairs room, and she complained and quarreled with the help more than ever. As her mind wandered, she even imagined that someone was trying to murder her.

Jack waited on Mrs. Moore with a gentleness and patience that Warren and many friends considered saintly. To stay with her, he gave up vacations, including trips to Ireland. In December 1947 he wrote Owen Barfield, "Things were never worse at the Kilns." He ended the letter by blaming his own attitude: "Of course the real trouble is within. All things would be bearable if I were delivered from this internal storm . . . of self-pity, rage, envy, terror, horror and general bilge!"

In his academic career, Jack had to endure setbacks. He was a conscientious tutor and a brilliant lecturer; he was widely respected by other scholars for his writings on English literature. By rights he should have been awarded a permanent chair, or professorship. If Jack became a professor, he would no longer have to tutor pupils, and he would have extra time for the study and writing that he loved.

But too many of his colleagues at Oxford disliked Jack for his outspokenness as a Christian and his success as a popular writer. Also, many of them had been offended by Jack's frank opinions of their own work. When elections for this or that "chair" came up, not enough senior faculty were willing to vote for him, so Oxford did not give C. S. Lewis a professorship.

In the midst of these troubles, pictures of another world were popping up in Jack's mind. *The Lion, the Witch and the Wardrobe,* he explained later, "all began with a picture of a Faun carrying an umbrella and parcels in a snowy wood. . . . At first I had very little idea how the story would go. But then suddenly Aslan came bounding into it. . . . Once He was there He pulled the whole story together, and soon He pulled the six other Narnian stories in after Him."

Hardly anyone who knew Jack in the late 1940s would have expected him to become a beloved children's author. One good friend, an early pupil, said afterward that "in all my acquaintance with [Jack] he never revealed his imaginative side." Even Mrs. Moore and Maureen (by this time married to Leonard Blake, the music teacher at Malvern College), who had lived with Jack for over twenty years, were astonished when he announced one day, "I think I'm going to write a children's book." He had never doted on little children the way Mrs. Moore did, and she had the impression that he didn't understand children.

But the important thing was that Jack had never lost touch with the child in himself, although he did not share this side of himself with many people. He and Warren still read children's books. Some of Jack's favorites, like Kenneth Grahame's *The Wind in the Willows,* he had discovered after he became an adult. Later, Jack would explain that in order to write a good children's story, you must "meet children as equals." As an example, he told the story of how he once exclaimed in a hotel dining room, "I loathe prunes." A six-year-old at a nearby table piped up: "So do I."

"Sympathy was instantaneous," Jack wrote. "Neither of us thought it funny. We both knew that prunes are far too nasty to be funny."

Cecil Harwood, a friend of Jack's since they were students together at Oxford, noticed the same natural sympathy between Jack and his children. They adored him. The learned C. S. Lewis would play games with the children, swing on their swing with them, swim with them, and draw pictures as if he were back with Warnie, long ago, at Little Lea.

During World War II, one of the children who stayed at the Kilns had been fascinated with the old, dark oak wardrobe stand-

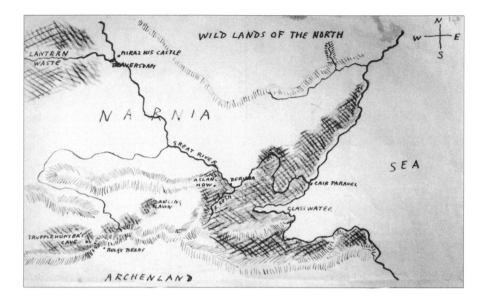

Map of Narnia, drawn by C. S. Lewis

ing in the hall. It was the same wardrobe that had been carved by Jack's Grandfather Lewis, and that Jack and Warnie had crawled into at Little Lea to tell stories. Was there a way out of the back of the wardrobe? the refugee child had wanted to know. And what was on the other side?

Now Jack saw that there could be a whole alternate universe, including the magical land of Narnia, on the other side of the wardrobe. This would fit nicely with the story he had started, several years ago, about four children who come to the countryside during the war. The old professor they stay with would be something like Jack's tutor, Kirkpatrick. And he would live in a house something like Little Lea, a large, rambling house "that you never seem to come to the end of . . . full of unexpected places." The most unexpected place in the house would be the wardrobe itself, through which the children would enter Narnia.

Although there was food rationing in England, Jack imagined feasting in Narnia. When Lucy arrives in Narnia in Chapter 2, she soon finds herself sitting down to tea with Mr. Tumnus the Faun. "A nice brown egg, lightly boiled, for each of them," wrote Jack with relish, "and then sardines on toast, and then buttered toast, and then toast with honey, and then a sugar-topped cake."

Early in 1949, Jack read the first two chapters of his story to J. R. R. Tolkien. He expected encouragement and understanding. Jack and "Tollers," as the Inklings called him, passionately agreed that stories, especially stories of the imagination, were very important. They agreed that myths conveyed a truth more real than the "real world." They also agreed that the modern world badly needed stories with the power of myths.

When Tolkien created the mythical world of Middle-earth in *The Hobbit* and *The Lord of the Rings,* Jack was one of his most enthusiastic fans. He had encouraged Tolkien to keep writing over the years — unlike Jack, Tolkien was a slow, painstaking writer. Jack had praised Tolkien's writing lavishly in conversations with friends and in reviews. Tolkien, for his part, had been "enthralled" by Jack's science-fiction novel *Out of the Silent Planet,* and he was even more admiring of *Perelandra.*

Given this background, Jack must have been shocked that Tolkien did not like his first children's book. In fact, Tolkien thoroughly disapproved of Narnia.

What bothered him so much was that Jack had not labored, as Tolkien had, to construct his imaginary world from the bottom up and make it perfectly consistent. Instead, Jack had joyfully mixed together all the different mythologies and different kinds of magical beings that were so vivid in his imagination. In Narnia, fauns of ancient Greek mythology live side by side with knights from the

Middle Ages, with talking beavers like the animals in *The Wind in the Willows,* and even with Father Christmas. And into this world of mixed-up magic Jack brought Lucy, an ordinary schoolgirl from modern London.

Jack couldn't see anything wrong with this. From the time he was a boy, he had felt that he was living in more than one world, and that unknown worlds might be "just around the corner." As he had the Professor declare in *The Lion, the Witch and the Wardrobe,* "Nothing is more probable."

Jack was hurt and discouraged by Tolkien's disapproval, but he couldn't let it stop him from writing this particular story. As he said some years later, he felt it was "exactly what I must write — or burst." So Jack went to Roger Lancelyn Green for a second opinion. Green, a former pupil and friend, had written a children's book on which Jack had advised and encouraged him a few years before. After listening to the first two chapters of *The Lion, the Witch and the Wardrobe,* Green assured Jack that it was good — more than good.

Afterward, Roger Green happened to see Tolkien, who said to him, "I hear you've been reading Jack's children's story. It really won't do, you know!"

Green didn't agree. He saw what Tolkien meant about the mixed mythologies, and he tried to get Jack to leave Father Christmas out of the story. But he thought the story was "one that could rank with the great ones of its kind."

Perhaps because of Tolkien's harsh criticism, Jack did not read *The Lion, the Witch and the Wardrobe* to the Inklings as he worked on it. By himself, he imagined and wrote about Narnia, a country under the spell of an evil witch. Jack poured everything he cared most about into Narnia.

He put in Mrs. Moore as kind, hospitable Mrs. Beaver, who

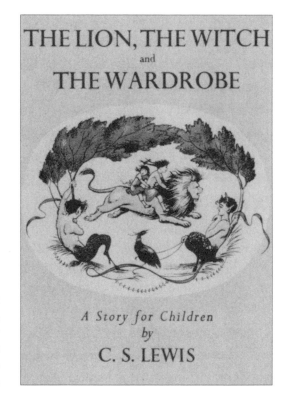

Lewis's first children's book was the classic work *The Lion, the Witch, and the Wardrobe*. Many people thought its publication would ruin his reputation as a serious adult writer.

wants to lug along her sewing machine when the beavers and the children are fleeing for their lives from the Witch. He put in the ways of medieval chivalry, which, readers are told at the end of the book, Peter and Susan and Edmund and Lucy live out for many years. The druids' stones that had thrilled his imagination at Avebury, he put in as the Stone Table of Deep Magic. Most important, he put in his sense of what the Son of God is like. As Christians believe that the world was rescued by Jesus Christ, Narnia would be rescued by the huge, beautiful, terrifying lion Aslan.

Jack asked Roger Green to read the completed story. With Green's enthusiastic encouragement, he then sent it to his publisher, Geoffrey Bles. Bles was reluctant to publish it, because he thought a children's book might hurt Jack's reputation as a serious writer. But he suggested that if Jack were determined to publish *The Lion, the Witch and the Wardrobe,* it would be better if he wrote a whole series of stories.

Eager to return to Narnia, in the spring of 1949 Jack began a new story. He started with a detail from the first book — the lamp-post that Lucy found in the wood outside the wardrobe. How did something as modern and ordinary as a lamppost get into Narnia? Jack made a start with this story, imagining a boy named Digory, and Polly, the girl next door, and Digory's godmother, a sorceress named Mrs. Lefay.

But there was something difficult about this story, and Jack didn't make much progress. Roger Green agreed with him that the story didn't seem to be going in the right direction. In June, worn out by work and family troubles, Jack was rushed to the hospital with a severe case of pneumonia. Warren was badly frightened, and he agreed with Dr. Havard that Jack should take a long vacation as soon as he recovered.

After a week in the hospital, Jack was much better, and hopefully he planned a month's visit with Arthur Greeves in Ireland. But it all depended on whether Warren could look after Mrs. Moore and the Kilns while he was gone. "It [would] be better if the door of my prison had never been opened than if it now bangs in my face!" Jack wrote Arthur. "How hard to submit to God's will." Only two days before Jack was due to leave for Ireland, Warren was drinking heavily, and Jack had to cancel his vacation.

Jack escaped not to Ireland but to Narnia, writing the story that would become *Prince Caspian.*

Lewis working on his papers at his study desk

CHAPTER 10

EXPLORING NARNIA

FOR JACK LEWIS, as he explained it later, writing stories was something like birdwatching. "I see pictures. Some of these pictures have a common flavour, almost a common smell, which groups them together. Keep quiet and watch and they will begin joining themselves up."

What came to Jack first, in writing *Prince Caspian,* was a picture of the four brothers and sisters of *The Lion, the Witch and the Wardrobe* being pulled into Narnia. They have been summoned, as they will find out, by a magic horn. Jack imagined Peter, Susan, Edmund, and Lucy being spirited off to Narnia from a train station, on their way to school. Maybe he was remembering his own school days and the many times, on the train to Wynyard or Malvern, when he would have been glad for something like that to happen to him.

From the moment they arrive in Narnia, the children are

launched on a quest. Their journey through the forests and over the water and down the cliffs of Narnia is like one of Jack's walking tours with his friends, only more exciting. The children get hot and thirsty and hungry; they argue and criticize and sometimes lose their tempers with each other. One of their first discoveries is a ruined castle, similar to medieval castles Jack had seen in Ireland and England. It turns out to be Cair Paravel, the former site of the Narnian court.

Since the Boxen days, Jack had loved to imagine characters with combined animal and human qualities. Now, in *Prince Caspian,* he populated the countryside with such creatures. The Prince's many loyal animal followers include the kind, steady old badger Trufflehunter, the wooly-voiced, snuffly Bulgy Bears, and the hyperactive squirrel Pattertwig. Best of all, Jack merged two of his old loves, "dressed animals" and medieval knights, in Reepicheep, the brave and courtly leader of the Talking Mice.

In addition to its familiar animals, Narnia was full of mythical creatures — centaurs, fauns, dwarves, giants. The most vivid, in *Prince Caspian,* are the tree-people. Jack had always had a deep feeling for trees. He could imagine the "soft, showery" voice of a birch; he could imagine how trees would dance in the moonlight, wading through the earth the way humans wade through water.

One of Jack's firmest convictions was that there is an ongoing struggle between good and evil. This is as true in *Prince Caspian* as in *The Lion, the Witch and the Wardrobe.* Peter and Susan and Edmund and Lucy find Narnia ruled by a new usurper, Caspian's uncle Miraz. Furthermore, Caspian's and Aslan's enemies include not only the troops of Miraz but also the friends of the White Witch. The forces of good include not only most of the talking animals but a whole wood of Awakened Trees, who rush at the enemy and force

Roger Lancelyn Green, the first enthusiastic supporter of
The Lion, the Witch and the Wardrobe

them to surrender.

Meanwhile, in Jack's real life, the fellowship of writers called the Inklings dwindled away. The core of the group — Jack and "Tollers" sharing their writing with their friends — no longer worked in the same way. Jack did not read aloud his Narnia stories, because he knew that Tolkien couldn't stand Narnia. And Tolkien had stopped reading aloud his own work-in-progress, *The Lord of the Rings,* because another Inkling, Hugo Dyson, let it be known

Pauline Baynes, illustrator of the Narnia books

that he was heartily bored by it.

The last Thursday meeting, a ham supper in Jack's rooms at Magdalen, took place in October 1949. Even before that, the meetings had become more about conversation than reading and criticism. The men were still friends, and they still met at the Eagle and Child on Tuesdays to talk — but it was not the same.

Jack finished *Prince Caspian* by December 1949. Again, Jack asked Roger Green to read it, and Green made minor suggestions. By this time, Pauline Baynes, who had illustrated Tolkien's *Farmer Giles of Ham,* was chosen to illustrate *The Lion, the Witch and the*

Wardrobe.

In rapid succession, between the beginning of 1950 and March of 1951, Jack wrote *The Voyage of the Dawn Treader, The Horse and His Boy,* and *The Silver Chair.* He showed the manuscripts to Roger Green, who made some small suggestions, but for the most part, Jack worked by himself. Using a "dip" pen and bottle of ink (which he often spilled, according to Maureen), Jack wrote quickly, without much revision. He threw away his first drafts, and even his final manuscripts after a book had been published, so there is not much evidence about how each story evolved.

But there is plenty of "evidence" about Jack himself in the Chronicles of Narnia. In these stories, he merged all the widely separated parts of his life, real and imaginary. Like Boxen, Narnia is on the seacoast, and like Belfast, Cair Paravel is at the mouth of a river. In the third book about Narnia, *The Voyage of the Dawn Treader,* Jack combined a group of friends on a quest with a sea voyage — a voyage in a dragon-prowed, single-masted craft, like the ship that the hero of *Beowulf* sailed to Denmark.

The gruesome nightmares that had plagued Jack when he was younger resurface in "The Dark Island," a chapter of *The Voyage of the Dawn Treader.* The voyagers discover a place "where dreams come true" — their *worst* dreams. Also, in this book the least likeable side of Jack as a boy appears as Eustace Scrub, a know-it-all little twerp heartily disliked by Lucy and Edmund. Eustace's selfishness and greediness turn him into a hideous dragon, and he needs Aslan's help to become human again.

Reepicheep, the leader of the Talking Mice who helps Caspian win back Narnia in the second book, reappears as one of the adventurers in *The Voyage of the Dawn Treader.* Although the valiant, courtly mouse is a comic character, he is also the one who achieves his heart's desire: to reach Aslan's country. The others only glimpse it. The hint of this country that comes to Eustace, Edmund, and Lucy on the breeze from the "utter east" is like Jack's "Joy" — happiness so intense that it could break your heart.

The next story Jack wrote, *The Horse and His Boy,* is about Shasta, an orphan boy who grows up in Calormen, a land south of Narnia. With the help of a talking horse, the boy runs away from his unkind foster father and heads for the mysterious north. After perilous adventures in the capital of Calormen and in the desert and the mountains on the way to Narnia, Shasta discovers who his real human father was. Better still, he knows his spiritual father, someone mightier and more loving than he could have dreamed of — Aslan.

Jack had always been fascinated with giants, and these creatures appear frequently in Narnia. Even good giants, like lovable, dim-witted Wimbleweather in *Prince Caspian,* are frightening, as well-meaning adults can be to a child. In *The Horse and His Boy,* Shasta's first reaction to the sight of six giants in the Narnian army is terror: "Though he knew they were on the right side Shasta could hardly bear to look at them; there are some things that take a lot of getting used to."

The next Narnia book Jack wrote, *The Silver Chair,* has even more to do with giants, but it begins with Eustace Scrub and a girl named Jill at boarding school in England. Like Jack's old school Malvern, their school is dominated by bullies, and the bullies are after them. Calling on Aslan for help, Jill and Eustace find a door and step through it, "out of the school grounds, out of England, out of our whole world."

The Silver Chair introduces one of Jack's most memorable creatures, Puddleglum the Marshwiggle, Jill and Eustace's guide on

F. W. Paxford, Lewis's gardener for thirty-four years. Puddleglum,
one of the major characters in *The Silver Chair*, is modeled after Paxford.

their quest. He is sort of a combination of a frog and Paxford, the
loyal, cheerfully gloomy gardener at the Kilns. It is Puddleglum, finally, who saves the day at the darkest moment of the story.

The adventure of Puddleglum, Eustace, and Jill includes ele-
ments of Jack's winter of hardship and danger during World War I.
Journeying on foot through the Wild Lands of the North, the

children and the Marshwiggle sleep on stony ground. They are cold and hungry and footsore. They are in mortal danger from giants, who throw boulders and deafen the travelers with their quarreling, and who shake the earth "like a bomb" when they jump.

The children's quest in *The Silver Chair* is to rescue Prince Rilian, heir to the throne of Narnia, who has been under an evil spell for years. This story has echoes of Jack's youth, recalling the years that he felt estranged from his best self. The enchanted prince is convinced by the evil Queen of the Underworld that all the important things in life — "trees and grass and sun and moon and stars and Aslan himself" — are only make-believe. But after a heroic action by Puddleglum, he and Rilian and the children are able to defeat the Queen. They return in triumph to Narnia, and then Jill and Eustace return to their school and give the bullies a taste of their own medicine.

✥ ✥ ✥ ✥

In April 1950, Mrs. Moore, now senile, had to be put into a nursing home. For several months Jack visited her every day. Although he was glad that Mrs. Moore seemed happier than she had in some time, it was painful for him to see his dear adopted mother with her mind "almost completely gone," as he wrote Sister Penelope. In January 1951, Mrs. Moore died of influenza. At last, Jack was relieved of the burden of caring for his adopted mother.

That spring, Jack returned to the story he had started before *Prince Caspian*. He saw that Digory could be the Professor of *The Lion, the Witch and the Wardrobe* as a boy. Digory's story, then (finally titled *The Magician's Nephew*), would take place in the time of Jack's own childhood. In fact, Jack drew on his childhood memories to create the details of the story. Like Little Lea, the house where Digory lives is a good place for indoor exploring. Polly, Digory's friend, even has a private corner in her attic like "the little end room," which she calls her "smugglers' cave."

Jack expressed his mystical feeling for trees again in *The Magician's Nephew*, first in his description of the "Wood Between the Worlds." This is the magical place that connects our world with other worlds such as Narnia. It is an intensely quiet place, so still that you can "almost feel the trees drinking the water up with their roots." Later in the story, after Aslan creates Narnia, he plants a tree for the protection of Narnia, a tree whose "spreading branches seemed to cast a light rather than a shade, and silver apples peeped out like stars from every leaf." The very smell of its apples is "joy and life and health."

Digory's mother, like young Jack's, is ill and expected to die. And like Jack, Digory asks for a miracle. Unlike young Jack, Digory is finally granted the miracle and a happy ending in this world.

But for the adult Jack, perhaps the best part of this story was the moment in which Digory realizes that the mighty and terrible Lion shares his grief. Aslan gives Digory the chance to confess what he has done wrong. And then he blesses Digory with a Lion's kiss of strength and courage.

In Jack's letters of the spring of 1951, written while he was writing *The Magician's Nephew,* he sounds positively joyous. Making arrangements to visit Arthur in Ireland, he exulted, "I know now how a bottle of champagne feels while the wire is being taken off the cork."

While Mrs. Moore was dying, Jack had undergone intense and troubling emotions. He grieved, of course, at losing his adopted mother, at the same time that he felt guilty for being relieved of the burden of caring for her. He felt sad, and perhaps guilty, too, that he had never helped her to a faith in God. In fact, her jealousy of his faith may have hindered her conversion. No doubt he also remembered his painful estrangement from his father during his first years with Mrs. Moore. And the death of his adopted mother must have reawakened the deepest sorrow of his life: the death of his real mother when he was nine.

A few months after Mrs. Moore's death, this emotional turmoil seems to have been resolved, and Jack felt himself in a new stage of closeness to God. In June 1951, he wrote to Sister Penelope about how "marvelously well" his life seemed now. "Indeed (I do not know whether to be ashamed or joyful at confessing this) I realize that until about a month ago, I never really believed (tho' I thought I did) in God's forgiveness."

In *The Magician's Nephew,* Jack described how Narnia had been created. In the seventh and final book, *The Last Battle,* he told of the end of Narnia. This book has a darker feeling than any of the others. The talking trees are slaughtered for timber; the Dwarfs lose faith in Aslan and turn against their king; and the citizens of Narnia are enslaved by the ruthless neighboring Calormenes.

Worst of all, it seems that Aslan has *caused* all this. "Would it not be better to be dead," says King Tirian, "than to have this horrible fear that Aslan has come and is not like the Aslan we have believed in and longed for?" But the despair that Tirian and his friends feel makes the end of the story all the brighter. They find themselves, for good, in Aslan's country, which includes everything and everyone they loved in both Narnia and England.

"The dream has ended," Aslan tells the children in the last chapter. "This is the morning."

✢ ✢ ✢ ✢

Jack Lewis believed, as his friend J. R. R. Tolkien believed, that whatever is worthwhile in the creative works of human beings comes from God. Especially in creating myths, a storyteller is reflecting (although of course in an imperfect way) God's truth. As a writer, Jack did not think of himself as "bringing into existence beauty or wisdom which did not exist before." Rather, he was trying to represent the beauty and wisdom that he had found in his life — that God had given to him.

George Sayer, a friend of Jack's who wrote a biography of him, feels that "the Narnia stories reveal more about Jack's personal religion than any of his theological books." As Jack explained later, it was Aslan the Christ-like lion who pulled the first Narnia book together and then inspired the other six books. In describing Aslan, Jack could describe his own experience of the Son of God.

In each of the seven books, there is a moment when the children meet Aslan. It is an awe-inspiring moment, because the Lion is "so bright and real and strong that everything else began at once to look pale and shadowy compared with him." No one can keep secrets from him — he knows them better than they know themselves. "They felt as glad as anyone can who feels afraid," wrote Jack in *Prince Caspian,* "and as afraid as anyone can who feels glad." Like everything about him, Aslan's voice is beautiful and frightening at the same time — "a sort of heavy, golden voice," thinks Jill in *The Silver Chair.*

For Digory and Polly in *The Magician's Nephew,* knowing and loving Aslan makes them feel reborn: "Such a sweetness and power rolled about them . . . that they felt they had never really been happy or wise or good, or even alive and awake, before."

George Sayer,
a favorite pupil of
Lewis's at Oxford, eventually
became headmaster of Malvern
College where Lewis attended
school as a boy.

✣ ✣ ✣ ✣

Jack's first children's book, *The Lion, the Witch and the Wardrobe,* was published in 1950. Many adult reviewers judged it too unrealistic, or too religious, or too frightening for children. But Jack believed it would give a child a false impression of life not to show that he or she "is born into a world of death, violence, wounds, adventure, heroism and cowardice, good and evil."

Children themselves loved *The Lion, the Witch and the Wardrobe.* They were just as eager as Jack had been to return to Narnia again and again. By 1956, all seven of the Chronicles of Narnia were in print.

Many children must have felt like George Sayer's stepdaughter did when she finished the last book. "I don't want to go on living in this world," she sobbed. "I want to live in Narnia with Aslan."

Thousands of readers wrote to Jack, and he always wrote back. To the many children who pleaded for more Narnia stories, he replied cheerfully but firmly. "As for doing more Narnian books than 7, isn't it better to stop when people are still asking for more than to go on till they are tired?"

Jack admired the pictures that children sent him of scenes from the Narnia books, and he commented on their stories and poems. He chatted with them about daily life: "I can never at present get my whole head & shoulders under water in my bath. (I like getting down like a Hippo with only my nostrils out)." "I have done lots of dish-washing in my time and I have often been read to, but I never thought of your very sensible idea of doing both together. How many plates do you smash in a month?"

Questions about writing and his Christian faith he answered seriously. "You are mistaken," he wrote to a fifth-grade class in Maryland, "when you think that everything in the books 'represents' something in this world. . . . I did not say to myself 'Let us represent Jesus as He really is in our world by a Lion in Narnia': I said 'Let us *suppose* that there were a land like Narnia and that the Son of God, as He became a Man in our world, became a Lion there, and then imagine what would happen.' If you think about it, you will see that it is quite a different thing." He added, simply and humbly, "When you say your prayers sometimes ask God to bless me."

In one long letter he replied to the mother of a boy who was worried because he liked Jack's Aslan, the Christ-like lion, better than he liked Jesus. "Laurence can't really love Aslan more than Jesus, even if he feels that's what he is doing. For the things he loves

Aslan for doing or saying are simply the things Jesus really did and said."

The next year, Jack answered a letter from Laurence himself. "Yes, people do find it hard to keep on feeling as if you believed in the next life: but then it is just as hard to keep on feeling as if you believed you were going to be nothing after death. I know this because in the old days before I was a Christian I used to try."

Hundreds of adults still wrote to Jack, too. One of the ones with whom Jack enjoyed corresponding was an American woman, Joy Davidman Gresham. Mrs. Gresham's letters, as Warren noted in his diary, were "amusing and well-written." She was a friend of Chad Walsh, the American critic who had visited Jack at Oxford in 1948. With Walsh's encouragement, she first wrote to Jack in 1950 about some religious questions.

Like Jack, Joy was a writer. Like Jack, she had converted to Christianity as an adult, partly because of reading his books. And like Jack, she loved a good knock-down, drag-out argument. As she told Chad Walsh, she thoroughly enjoyed Jack's first reply to her, in which the "master of debate" shot down all her arguments "fair and square."

After Joy and Jack had gotten to know each other through letters, she came to England in the fall of 1952.

Joy Davidman Gresham as a young woman

CHAPTER 11

JOY AND A MIRACLE

JOY DAVIDMAN GRESHAM and Jack Lewis first met, at her invitation, for lunch at a hotel. She was an attractive, dark-haired, well-dressed woman of thirty-seven. Her conversation in person was as lively and intelligent as her letters, and Jack laughed heartily at her wit.

In turn, Jack invited Joy to lunch at Magdalen College with Warren and some of Jack's friends. Warren was a bit taken aback by Joy's New York brashness, but he liked her, too. That Christmas, Jack and Warren invited Joy to the Kilns for two weeks.

Joy had come to England in part to decide whether she ought to stay in her unhappy marriage to Bill Gresham. As a Christian, she felt that divorce was wrong; but her husband did not seem committed to either Christianity or their marriage. Furthermore, Bill was sometimes drunken and violent. Joy hoped to get help from "one of the clearest thinkers of our time" — C. S. Lewis. During the Christmas visit, Joy told Jack about her dilemma and showed him a letter from her husband, asking for a divorce. Jack advised her to divorce him.

Back in New York shortly after Christmas, Joy became more convinced than ever that her marriage was over. In November 1953, she left her husband and returned to London to live. She brought along her two boys, David (nine and a half) and Douglas (eight), who loved the Narnia books. The boys first met Jack in December, on a visit with their mother to the Kilns.

At first Douglas was disappointed that the author of the magical Narnia books did not look like "a cross between Sir Galahad and Merlin the Wise." As Jack had written to the fifth-graders in Maryland, "I'm tall, fat, rather bald, red-faced, double-chinned, black-haired, have a deep voice, and wear glasses for reading."

But Douglas got over his disappointment, and the Gresham boys explored the woods and hills around the Kilns with Jack. When they left to return to London, Jack let them take the manuscript of one of his not-yet-published Narnia books, *The Horse and His Boy,* so that they could read it right away. He dedicated that book to David and Douglas.

Jack and Joy became close friends. They had a great deal in common, in spite of the fact that she was a woman from a New York Jewish background and he was a man from Protestant Belfast. They both loved to argue for fun, fighting hard but with good humor. They both delighted in language — sometimes they would play Scrabble in several languages at once.

Perhaps most important, they each understood the mystical side of the other's Christian faith. For instance, Joy could accept Jack's experience of feeling his friend Charles Williams's presence after his death in 1945. And Jack could understand Joy's story about

Jack with Joy Davidman's sons, David (left) and Douglas (right)

the night of her conversion, when she sensed "a Person with me in that room . . . a Person so real that all my precious life was by comparison mere shadow play."

C.S. Lewis

Joy had written poems and two novels, and she had recently finished *Smoke on the Mountain: An Interpretation of the Ten Commandments* — dedicated to C. S. Lewis. Jack had advised her on this book, and they generally read and critiqued each other's writing. One of Jack's books that Joy read before publication was his autobiography, which he finished in 1955. Its title, *Surprised by Joy,* comes from a poem by one of Jack's favorite poets, William Wordsworth.

In his preface, Jack warned the reader that *Surprised by Joy* was the story of his conversion, not a general autobiography. Therefore, it would not include *all* the important facts about his life. He did not mention Mrs. Moore, his adopted mother, with whom he had lived for over thirty years, except to hint that "one huge and complex episode will be omitted."

Likewise, Jack did not mention his father's death, except to claim that it "does not really come into the story I am telling." Jack's friend and physician, Dr. Havard, commented that there was a great deal missing from the autobiography. Jokingly he threatened to fill in the gaps by writing a book called *Suppressed by Jack.*

When his autobiography came into print in September 1955, Jack was at work on a new novel for adults, finally titled *Till We Have Faces.* It was based on a Greek myth about a young woman, Psyche, who falls in love with the god Eros. Jack had been fascinated by this myth ever since he was a boy, and he had thought of writing a poem about Psyche's sister as early as 1923. Now, with Joy's encouragement and criticism, he retold the myth as the story of Orual, Psyche's older sister.

Through this story, set in the imaginary kingdom of Glome, Jack revisited the most painful parts of his childhood. Orual's mother dies when she is young; her father, the king, is a brutal tyrant; the only person who acts like a loving parent to her is her Greek tutor.

144

When Orual loses her beloved younger sister, she loses all faith. "The gods are real," she rails, "and viler than the vilest men."

Orual's story confronts the painfulness of human love and the human struggle to accept God's love. Some critics have suggested that Orual, an ugly woman who covers her face with a veil, represents Jack's inmost feelings about himself. Jack's empathy with strong, assertive Orual seems also to reflect his closeness to Joy Davidman, and he dedicated the book to her.

Jack thought *Till We Have Faces,* published in 1956, was his best work of fiction. A few others, including Joy herself and Jack's old friend Owen Barfield, agreed with him. But the tone of this novel was harsh and bleak. Most of the devoted C. S. Lewis fans who loved *The Screwtape Letters* and the Chronicles of Narnia did not like it at all.

Meanwhile, Joy's divorce had become final in August 1954. The next summer she and her sons had moved to a house in Headington, within walking distance of the Kilns. She planned to stay in England permanently. By this time, Jack had taken on an almost fatherly responsibility for David and Douglas. He gave David lessons in Latin, and he paid for the boys' education at a private school. He also bought the boys books and toys. He even kept a pony at the Kilns for them to ride.

Early in 1956, the British government refused to renew Joy's permit to live in England. She and the boys would have to leave — unless she married a British citizen. Deeply concerned for them, Jack married Joy in a civil ceremony, which took place in April 1956 at the Oxford registry office.

This civil marriage was just a formality to allow Joy and her sons to stay in England, Jack explained to his friend George Sayer. To both Jack and Joy, the only real marriage was a Christian

Jack and Joy in 1958, when her cancer was in remission. Jack was
astonished by — and grateful for — the love he shared with Joy.

marriage. They did not consider themselves husband and wife, and
they continued to live apart.

That was as far as their relationship went — until October
1956, when it was suddenly discovered that Joy was very ill. She
broke her thighbone merely by falling to the floor, and X-rays at
the hospital showed advanced bone cancer. The doctors gave her
only a short time to live.

Joy longed to come "home" to the Kilns to die, and Jack
wanted her to, but they felt they ought to be married as Christians
first. In March 1957 Jack asked Peter Bide, an Episcopal priest who
had a reputation for healing sick people through prayer, to come
and pray for Joy's recovery. When he came, Father Bide also married
Jack and Joy in her hospital room. Warren witnessed the ceremony,

and he wrote in his diary, "I found it heartrending . . . though to feel pity for anyone so magnificently brave as Joy is almost an insult."

The week after the marriage ceremony, Joy did come home to the Kilns. "I am newly married and to a dying woman," Jack had written earlier to one of his American correspondents. "Every moment is spent at her bedside." He asked for prayers "for help and guidance in the difficult responsibility of bringing up two orphan stepsons. I have only one qualification, if it is one: these two boys are now facing the same calamity that befell my brother and me at about their age."

But instead of dying, Joy began to get better. "There is little pain, often none, her strength increases, and she eats and sleeps well," Jack wrote Sister Penelope in May. ". . . Forbidden and torturing hopes *will* intrude (on us both). In short, a dungeon is never harder to bear than when the door is opened and the sunshine & birdsongs float in. Pray hard for us both, dear sister."

By June, Jack was openly in love and hoping for a miracle. "The situation is not easy to describe," he wrote a friend. "My heart is breaking and I was never so happy before: at any rate there is more in life than I knew about." By a strange coincidence, his love for this woman, Joy, was like the feeling of "Joy" that he had pursued in his pre-Christian days: an almost unbearable mixture of happiness and grief.

Joy, too, told a visiting friend about the love between her and Jack: "The movies and the poets are right: it does exist!"

Around this time, a former student of Jack's ran into Jack and Joy when they were out for lunch together. He was surprised at how mellow and relaxed Jack seemed in Joy's company. He sensed that Joy brought out a sensitive inner Jack that few other people knew.

Joy continued to recover. By November 1957 she was limping around with a cane. By early 1958 she was supervising the repair and redecoration of the Kilns, which was badly needed. The blackout curtains from World War II were still up, and the house was in such a mess that the Lewis brothers' friends called it "the Midden" (Middle English for "trash heap"). The structure was so decayed that a chunk of the ceiling of Douglas's bedroom fell down, nearly on top of him.

Besides overseeing repairs to the house, Joy defended the grounds, as fierce as Orual the warrior queen in *Till We Have Faces*. She once ordered a trespasser, armed with a bow and arrow, off the property at the point of a shotgun. She also managed Jack's finances, which were as neglected as his house. With his lifelong block against mathematics, he had not even realized that his money should be in a savings account, earning interest, rather than a checking account.

Outside of Jack's early childhood years, this may have been the happiest time of his life. As he remarked to his friend Nevill Coghill in the summer of 1958, "I never expected to have, in my sixties, the happiness that passed me by in my twenties." Fittingly, during the spring of that year Jack was working on a new series of radio talks on the subject of four different aspects of love: affection, friendship, sexual love, and Christian love.

That July, Jack and Joy took a trip to Ireland, combining a honeymoon with a visit to Arthur Greeves. They decided to fly — the first airplane trip for both of them. As they were leaving for the airport, Paxford the gardener, in his most cheerfully gloomy Marshwiggle style, informed them of a news report. A plane had crashed. "Everybody killed — burnt beyond recognition."

In spite of Paxford's jolly warning, and in spite of Jack's dislike of modern inventions, the airplane ride was thrilling. In the

The Inver area, County Donegal, in Ireland

Narnia stories, Jack had imagined several times what it would be like to fly. The reality was just as exciting as Digory and Polly's ride on a winged horse in *The Magician's Nephew*.

"We found it, after one initial moment of terror, enchanting," he wrote a friend. "The cloud-scape seen from above is a new world of beauty. . . . We had clear weather over the Irish Sea and the first Irish headland, brightly sunlit, stood out from the dark sea (it's very dark when you're looking directly down on it) like a bit of enamel."

The sunny weather in Ireland held as Jack introduced Joy to his childhood friend, Arthur, and as they drove through the beautiful Carlingford Mountains of County Louth, so much like the mountains of Narnia. They explored County Down, south of Belfast, and finally County Donegal on the northern Atlantic coast. Jack loved showing Joy his Ireland, including the sights, such as the Mourne Mountains, which had first aroused his imagination. Joy thought Ireland was the most beautiful place she had ever seen. They returned, as Jack put it, "drunk with blue mountains, yellow beaches, dark fuchsia, breaking waves, braying donkeys, peat-smell, and the heather just then beginning to bloom."

But that fall Jack wrote Roger Green, "The cancer in the bones is awake again. . . . It is like being recaptured by the giant when you have passed every gate and are almost out of sight of his castle."

Although Joy was ill and in pain, she and Jack planned another trip. In April 1960 they flew to Greece, the land of the mythology and poetry and philosophy that they both loved. Joy even managed to climb the Acropolis, in Athens, to see the ruins of the Parthenon, the temple of Athena.

After the trip, Joy's health failed rapidly. On July 13, 1960, she died in the hospital with Jack by her side. Afterward, Jack wrote to Arthur Greeves,

> There were a couple of hours of atrocious pain on her last morning, but the rest of the day [she was] mostly asleep, tho' rational whenever she was conscious. Two of her last remarks were "You have made me happy" and "I am at peace with God." . . .
>
> Douglas — the younger boy — is, as always, an absolute brick, and a very bright spot in my life.

From the beginning, Jack had felt closer to Douglas than to his older brother, David. As Jack had written to Sister Penelope during Joy's first illness, David was "less engaging" and more like Jack himself at thirteen — a "bookworm, pedant, and a bit of a prig." In spite of Jack's efforts, he and David never became close.

Douglas was fourteen at the time of Joy's death. Long afterward, he remembered Jack "the evening after my mother died. It was the first time I ever saw a grown man cry. He put his arm around me, and I put mine around him, and we tried to comfort each other."

Many years earlier, Jack had written Arthur Greeves from Great Bookham, "Whenever you are fed up with life, start writing." Now, at the age of sixty-one, he took his own advice once more. The result was a *A Grief Observed,* a short, intense book, written as if it were a private diary. Jack described how his feelings and thoughts changed as he grieved for his wife and tried to understand what her death meant for his Christian faith.

At first, his grieving reads like screams of pain. "Go to [God] when your need is desperate, when all other help is vain, and what do you find? A door slammed in your face and a sound of bolting and double bolting on the inside. After that, silence."

To add to his pain, Jack is not able to comfort his stepsons — even Douglas is now embarrassed by Jack's open grief. Jack remembers sadly how, after his mother's death, he felt estranged from his own grief-stricken father.

Gradually Jack calms down, like someone recovering (to his surprise) from a high fever. He comes to believe that losing his loved one is not the end of his marriage but a normal stage in every marriage, to be followed by a growing spiritual rapport. He must let go of his earthly relationship with Joy in order to move on to the next stage.

Finally, Jack describes wonderingly the sensation of being in touch with Joy again. He has "the impression of her mind momentarily facing my own. . . . Not at all like a rapturous reunion of lovers. Much more like getting a telephone call or a wire from her about some practical arrangement."

Jack wanted to publish *A Grief Observed* in the hope of helping other sufferers. Still, he did not want readers to connect the book with his private life, and so it was first published under a pen name. Ever since then, this book has offered a message of hope: Even the strongest believers can go through agonies of doubt. And losing the most beloved person in your life does not mean that you have to lose God, too.

Once again, through writing, "the great cure for all human ills," Jack had transformed a personal struggle into a gift that would help many others with their own struggles.

Cambridge, England. Lewis would spend the last eight years of his life as Chair of Medieval and Renaissance English at Magdalene College, Cambridge.

CHAPTER 12

FAREWELL TO SHADOW-LANDS

C. S. LEWIS'S FANS WERE hoping for more books, especially Narnia books. As Jack's stepson Douglas put it, "When are you going to stop writing all this bilge [perhaps he meant *An Experiment in Criticism,* a book of literary criticism published in 1961] and write interesting books again?"

To one girl who wrote Jack in 1962, asking for more Narnia books, he suggested that she write stories herself "to fill up the gaps in Narnian history." He ended the letter by saying, "I feel *I* have done all I can!"

As long ago as 1953, writing *The Last Battle,* Jack had known that there would be no more Narnia books. In "Farewell to Shadow-Lands," the final chapter of the final Chronicle of Narnia, he had tried to explain this to his readers. "The things that began to happen after that were so great and beautiful that I cannot write them. And for us this is the end of all the stories. . . ."

The stories had begun with a picture: the faun with an umbrella and parcels in a snowy wood. Now there were no more pictures in his mind, Jack told George Sayer. No more intriguing images, like the mysterious back of the wardrobe or the lamppost in the woods, would "join themselves up" to form a new story.

Jack Lewis's life was drawing to an end. After caring for Joy while she was dying, he was exhausted. But Jack, with Warren's help, still answered letters from hundreds of readers. He still gave lectures, although now at Cambridge rather than Oxford. In 1954, he had been made a professor at Cambridge University, about eighty miles from Oxford.

Because he still lived at the Kilns, which was near Oxford, Jack commuted to Cambridge on the train every week. He often said his prayers while he was riding the train or walking up and down the platform at the station.

Clifford Morris, the taxi driver who regularly drove Jack to and from the Oxford train station — and sometimes all the way to or from Cambridge — remembered him from this time as a good friend and companion. He also remembered Jack's old tweed fisherman's hat. Once, when they stopped by the road on the way back from Cambridge to eat their sandwiches, Jack left his hat behind. Weeks later, he returned to the same place and found his hat under a hedge, with field mice living in it. He took the hat home (presumably removing the mice first) and wore it.

Only a year after Joy's death, Jack had become seriously ill: he had an enlarged prostate gland, and his kidneys were damaged. He needed surgery, but it was too dangerous to risk. His heart was weak — perhaps from a lifetime of heavy smoking.

In 1956, even before the great happiness and anguish of his marriage, Jack had written to his friend Alan Bede Griffiths, "It seems to me that one can hardly say anything either bad enough or good enough about life." Jack had suffered great hardships, including his mother's death and the massive slaughter of World War I. And he had enjoyed great blessings, including his friendships ("the chief happiness of life," he had once called them) and his worldwide fame as a Christian writer.

One of the darkest parts of Jack's life had been his two years at Wynyard School, just after his mother's death. Even after he grew up, Jack had hated the headmaster, Robert Capron, so much that he liked the thought of him suffering in hell. Then, after he became a Christian, Jack had tried over and over to forgive Capron. Now that Jack was sixty-four, he suddenly found that he actually *had* forgiven him. "And, like learning to swim or ride a bicycle," he wrote a friend, "the moment it does happen it seems so easy and you wonder why on earth you didn't do it years ago."

During his final three years, Jack lived at the Kilns with Warren in a quiet routine of reading and writing. His last book was *Letters to Malcolm: Chiefly on Prayer,* which he finished in May 1963. Some years earlier he had tried to work on a book about prayer, but it took form only after he decided to write it as letters. Jack was a superb letter-writer, whether he was addressing an imaginary "Malcolm" or a real person.

In *Letters to Malcolm,* Jack imagined what the "resurrection of the body" promised by Saint Paul might be like. It would *not,* he was sure, be "the soul re-assuming the corpse." He described how "the new earth and sky, the same yet not the same as these, will rise in us as we have risen in Christ. And once again, after who knows what aeons of silence and the dark, the birds will sing and the waters flow, and lights and shadows move across the hills, and the faces of our friends laugh upon us with amazed recognition."

This was how Jack imagined heaven, or "Aslan's country." As he described it in *The Last Battle,* it would have everything he loved in the natural world: blue sky and green grass, fruit trees and flowers, hills and mountains, sea and islands and breezes. Clothes would feel good as well as look good. He would meet all his friends again, human and animal, and join them in endless adventures. Heaven would be like Narnia, only better.

In July 1963, just when Jack was planning to visit Arthur Greeves in Belfast one more time, he had a heart attack and sank into a coma. He recovered, but he knew he didn't have long to live. "To be brought back and have all one's dying to do *again* was rather hard," complained Jack jokingly in a letter to Sister Penelope.

At this point, Jack resigned his professorship at Cambridge. With the help of Walter Hooper, a young American theologian, he sorted out his books and papers.

Warren wrote afterward in his diary about his brother's final weeks that fall. This time reminded him of the days when he and Jack were boys, after their mother died:

> Joy had left us, and once again — as in the earliest days — we could turn for comfort only to each other. The wheel had come full circle: once again we were together in the little end room at home, shutting out from our talk the ever-present knowledge that the holidays were ending, that a new term fraught with unknown possibilities awaited us both.

Jack Lewis's brother was the last person to see him alive. On Friday, November 22, 1963, Jack died in his room at the Kilns. (By coincidence, this was also the day that President John F. Kennedy

Headington Quarry Parish Church, Oxfordshire

was assassinated.) It was only a week before his sixty-fifth birthday.

Jack's funeral at his church, Holy Trinity in Headington Quarry, was kept private, at Warren's request. But Warren could not bring himself to attend the service. He must have been overcome by the same "sheer wave of animal panic" he had felt back in 1947 at the thought of losing his brother. He could not face "the prospect of the empty years" he had dreaded so long.

J. R. R. Tolkien and his son Christopher were at the funeral. As Tolkien wrote his daughter the next day, Jack's death had hit him "like an axe-blow near the roots" of an old tree. Some of the others present on this cold, bright, still morning were Owen Barfield, George Sayer, Jack's "adopted sister" Maureen and her husband Leonard Blake, Jack's stepsons David and Douglas Gresham, and

Fred Paxford, the model for Puddleglum the Marshwiggle.

As for Jack, for a long time he had held a vivid expectation of what this day would be like for *him*. Writing of old King Caspian's death in *The Silver Chair,* he had imagined what it might be like for the one who dies. At the same moment when Caspian's heartbroken friends are mourning him in Narnia, the Lion is awakening him to joyful new life — in Aslan's country.

✛ ✛ ✛ ✛

The day after Jack Lewis's death, Owen Barfield sat down to re-read his letters from his old friend. He expected a "solemn and mournful" experience. Instead, he found himself laughing out loud. Undoubtedly Jack would have been delighted.

Jack would have been glad, too, when his brother finally re-read his own diaries and enjoyed all over again the many "good times I had with the SPB [Small Pigiebotham]." Warren especially loved reading about the walking tours they had taken together. "I can see him almost as if he was visible, on a path in front of me, striding along with stick and pack in his shapeless old fisherman's hat."

Tolkien had written in his diary long ago, during a difficult period in his life, "Friendship with Lewis compensates for much." Now he realized, more than ever, how important Jack's encouragement had been to his writing. "An unpayable debt," he called it.

Alan Bede Griffiths, one of Jack's first students at Oxford, remembered that this brilliant scholar had always treated him as an equal. "I think that it was through him that I really discovered the meaning of friendship." Derek Brewer, a student of Jack's in the 1940s, remembered him roaring with laughter. He also recalled

Jack's grave at
Holy Trinity Church,
Headington Quarry,
Oxford. Admirers come
from all over the world to
visit this site.

Jack helping needy students, sometimes (although he never let them know it) from his own funds. Another student from the same period said, "What stands out in my mind is the warmth of the man."

Douglas Gresham, Jack's stepson, said that Jack was like a father to him — more than his own father was. One moment he especially liked to remember was the time he found Jack and his mother reading poetry together. They were so touched by the beauty of the words that tears were running down their faces.

As for the Inklings, all the men who had met in Jack's rooms on Thursday evenings would cherish the memory of that fellowship of Christian writers. But no one had taken more delight in the fellowship than Jack. The Inklings would not have flourished except for him, "the link that bound us together," as Dr. Havard put it.

And hundreds of letterwriters who had never met C. S. Lewis knew him as the man they trusted with their deepest religious and personal problems. They relied on him for counseling, almost as if he were a clergyman.

But Jack Lewis's influence didn't end with the people who knew him one way or another during his lifetime. In every generation, new readers discover his books. Thousands of people still enjoy Jack's humor. They find support in his reasoning about the Christian faith; C. S. Lewis is still honored as a champion explainer of Christianity. As one critic put it, "Lewis is the ideal persuader for the half-convinced, for the good man who would like to be a Christian but finds his intellect getting in the way."

Furthermore, readers are still transported by C. S. Lewis's imagination. Many would agree with Nevill Coghill that Jack's works of the imagination are likely to be his most enduring books. As Jack himself put it, a story "at its best . . . can give us experiences we have never had." Jack's own experiences in the world of the imagination had been some of the most important events of his life.

Praising George MacDonald, a Christian and mythmaker who had deeply influenced him, Jack had said, "Every now and then there occurs in the modern world a genius . . . who can make such a story." The Chronicles of Narnia alone are proof of Jack Lewis's own mythmaking genius.

✠ ✠ ✠ ✠

I once received a letter from a girl who said she had enjoyed reading my latest book — and incidentally, could I give her C. S. Lewis's address? I wasn't insulted that she was using me to get in touch with her *real* favorite author. He was my favorite, too. But for the same reason, I was sorry to be the one to give her the bad news: C. S. Lewis had died before she was born.

The good news is that Jack Lewis, although he does not live in Oxford at the Kilns anymore, is very much alive in his books. Jack is one of those authors who seems to make friends with his readers, just as in life he cherished his friends. "He had, indeed, a remarkable talent for friendship," wrote his brother, Warren.

Some of Jack Lewis's best friends were the authors of his favorite books. Now, we can get to know him by doing what Jack himself did with those authors — whether they had written hundreds of years ago or were still writing. He read all their books. Then he read them again. He wrote about their books; he talked about them; he used them to change his life.

Owen Barfield described what it was like when he got a letter from Jack Lewis: "You opened the envelope and you heard his voice." It's like that now, reading his books. You open the book and you hear his voice.

MY SOURCES FOR THIS BOOK

In writing this book, I drew on a number of valuable sources. The most important were C. S. Lewis's own writings, of course, including his fiction for children and adults, his autobiography, his diary, his letters, and collections of his talks and essays. Also vital were books about C. S. Lewis and those close to him, including *Brothers and Friends: The Diaries of Major Warren Hamilton Lewis,* edited by Clyde S. Kilby and Marjorie Lamp Mead; *C. S. Lewis: A Biography,* by Roger Lancelyn Green and Walter Hooper; *Jack: A Life of C. S. Lewis,* by George Sayer; *The Inklings: C. S. Lewis, J. R. R. Tolkien, Charles Williams, and Their Friends,* by Humphrey Carpenter; *C. S. Lewis at the Breakfast Table* (a collection of reminiscences by several people who knew him in various settings), edited by James T. Como; *And God Came In* (a biography of Joy Davidman Lewis), by Lyle W. Dorsett; and *Lenten Lands: My Childhood with Joy Davidman and C. S. Lewis,* by Douglas Gresham.

I am indebted to the Marion E. Wade Center at Wheaton College, where I saw the original wardrobe and read some unpublished papers related to C. S. Lewis. I thank the Wade Center's staff, especially Associate Director Marjorie Lamp Mead, co-editor of *Brothers & Friends* and of *Letters to Children.* She read the manuscript of my book and gave valuable advice for revising it. Other readers who contributed helpful suggestions were Steven R. Ayers, Hilary Ayers, and William Griffin, author of *Clive Staples Lewis: A Dramatic*

Life. Amy Eerdmans DeVries and Mary Hietbrink, my editors at Eerdmans, patiently guided me through more than one revision.

SUGGESTIONS FOR FURTHER READING

BOOKS BY C. S. LEWIS

The Chronicles of Narnia
(in the order in which the stories take place in Narnia):
    The Magician's Nephew (1955)
    The Lion, the Witch and the Wardrobe (1950)
    The Horse and His Boy (1954)
    Prince Caspian (1951)
    The Voyage of the Dawn Treader (1952)
    The Silver Chair (1953)
    The Last Battle (1956)
Wonderful reading — and perhaps the deepest expression of
Lewis's experience of God.

Lewis's science-fiction trilogy:
    Out of the Silent Planet (1938)
    Perelandra (1943)
    That Hideous Strength (1945)
Absorbing and thought-provoking novels about the struggle between good and evil, on an interplanetary stage. Just put out of your
mind what recent science has discovered about Mars and Venus.
Some readers may be disturbed by a few graphic descriptions, in
Perelandra and *That Hideous Strength,* of the perverse cruelty of the
evil beings. But these are compelling stories about imperfect human beings confronted with moral choices, written with splendid

imagining of worlds beyond the one we know.

Boxen: The Imaginary World of the Young C. S. Lewis
>   Edited by Walter Hooper. San Diego: Harcourt Brace
>   Jovanovich, 1985 (hardcover); 1986 (paperback).

A fascinating glimpse, through his stories and pictures, into Lewis's young imagination and developing creativity. But don't expect Narnia!

Letters to Children
>   Edited by Lyle W. Dorsett and Marjorie Lamp Mead.
>   New York: Macmillan, 1985 (hardcover).

Lewis's letters to fans of the Narnia books as well as to children he knew personally.

On Stories: And Other Essays on Literature by C. S. Lewis
>   Edited by Walter Hooper. New York: Harcourt Brace
>   Jovanovich, 1982 (hardcover and paperback).

A collection of talks and essays by Lewis, in which he explains how he wrote and how deeply he felt about stories, especially stories for children.

The Screwtape Letters (1942)

Lewis's playful and insightful comments on the struggle to lead a Christian life, written as senior devil Screwtape's diabolical advice to his nephew Wormwood.

Surprised by Joy (1955)

Lewis's autobiography, from his childhood to his conversion to Christianity. Some readers may be distressed by Lewis's description, in chapter 2, of the brutality of the headmaster of Wynyard,

Lewis's first school, or offended by Lewis's reference, in chapter 6, to homosexuality among the boys at Malvern College. But overall, the book is fascinating and inspiring. It gives a vivid picture of Lewis's early life and the people in it, especially of his father and his tutor, W. T. Kirkpatrick.

BOOKS ABOUT C. S. LEWIS

C. S. Lewis: Images of His World by Douglas Gilbert and Clyde S. Kilby.
    Grand Rapids: Wm. B. Eerdmans, 2005 (cloth).
An introduction to C. S. Lewis through a chronology of the main events in his life, a summary of his spiritual journey, and quotations from Lewis's writings that accompany a first-rate collection of photographs, many in color, of the places and people Lewis knew. It includes several of Lewis's own drawings and handwritten manuscript pages.

*The Inklings: C. S. Lewis, J. R. R. Tolkien, Charles Williams, and Their
    Friends* by Humphrey Carpenter. Boston: Houghton Mifflin,
    1979 (hardcover); New York: Ballantine Books, 1981 (paperback).
Based on many firsthand accounts, this biography describes in detail the group of Christian writers and friends who became known as the Inklings. Again, some passages about Lewis's private life may not be appropriate for young readers. But the book is an evocative portrait of this unique group of friends, describing their backgrounds and their life together at Oxford in the 1930s and 1940s.

Jack: A Life of C. S. Lewis by George Sayer. Wheaton, Ill.: Crossway
    Books, 1994 (paperback). This book was originally

published under the title *Jack: C. S. Lewis and His Times* by Harper & Row in 1988.

An affectionate but fair biography, using up-to-date sources, by a longtime friend (once a student) of C. S. Lewis. Some readers may not be ready for Sayer's discussion of the controversy over Lewis's relationship with Mrs. Moore, or of Lewis's guilt over his adolescent sexual feelings. But these are brief passages in an excellent biography, one of the most knowledgeable, thorough, and well written of the many books about Lewis.

ACKNOWLEDGMENTS

PHOTOGRAPHS

The photographs on pp. xii, 2, 5, 6, 10, 14, 18, 33, 36, 37, 39, 47, 53, 61, 75, 84, 89, 90, 95, 114, 116, 124, 140, 143 are from the Marion E. Wade Center, Wheaton College, Wheaton, Ill. Used by permission.

The photographs on pp. 19, 21, 34 are of illustrations by C. S. Lewis copyright © C. S. Lewis Pte. Ltd. All photographs are from the Marion E. Wade Center, Wheaton College, Wheaton, Ill. Used by permission.

The photograph on page 119 is of an illustration by C. S. Lewis copyright © C. S. Lewis Pte. Ltd. Used by permission of Bodleian Library, University of Oxford.

The photograph on page 122 is used with permission. *The Lion, the Witch and the Wardrobe* by C. S. Lewis copyright © C. S. Lewis Pte. Ltd 1950. Book cover used by permission of HarperCollins Publishers.

The photographs on pp. 17, 24, 26, 30, 34, 64, 67, 72, 76, 79, 87, 103, 106, 127, 128, 131, 136, 149, 154, 159 are by Douglas Gilbert. Used by permission.

The photograph on p. 44 is courtesy of The Master and Fellows of University College, Oxford.

The photographs on pp. 66 and 161 are by Stephen W. Mead. Both photographs are from The Marion E. Wade Center, Wheaton College,

Wheaton, Ill. Used by permission.

The photographs on p. ii and 100 are by Arthur Strong. Used by permission.

The photograph on p. 146 is by Michael Peto, courtesy of Dundee University Library, Department of Archives & Manuscripts.

The photographs on pp 41, 48, 51, 58 are supplied courtesy of the Library of Congress.

PUBLICATIONS

The author and publisher gratefully acknowledge permission granted to use the following materials:

Excerpts from *The Letters of C. S. Lewis.* Copyright © 1966 by W. H. Lewis and the Executors of C. S. Lewis and renewed 1994 by C. S. Lewis Pte. Ltd. Reprinted by permission of The C. S. Lewis Company (World excluding U.S.) and Harcourt Brace & Company (U.S.).

Excerpts from *Letters to Children* by C. S. Lewis. Copyright © 1985 by C. S. Lewis Pte. Ltd. Reprinted by permission of The C. S. Lewis Company (World excluding U.S.) and Simon & Schuster (U.S.).

Excerpts from *Surprised by Joy* by C. S. Lewis. Copyright © 1956 by C. S. Lewis Pte. Ltd. and renewed 1984 by Arthur Owen Barfield. Reprinted by permission of Harcourt Brace & Company (U.S. and Philippines) and The C. S. Lewis Company (world except U.S. and Philippines).

Excerpts from *They Stand Together: The Letters of C. S. Lewis to Arthur Greeves.* Copyright © 1979 by C. S. Lewis Pte. Ltd. Reprinted by permission of The C. S. Lewis Company.

INDEX